TEST YOUR N.Q.
(Nostalgia Quotient)

DENIS GIFFORD . . . SOUNDS FAMILIAR?

If the author's name sounds familiar, that's because it is. He has been running his radio panel game of the same name for six successful years – in fact, the current season will notch the score up to a century! Not bad for a show that nobody wanted. It took Denis Gifford three years hard labour to get his idea on the air – now everybody wants it! A visual version started on the box this autumn fathered by Thames Television – called 'Looks Familiar' of course, and now NEL proudly presents a paperback fun-book the whole family can join in.

Nostalgia, once a dirty word on the showbiz scene, is in with a bang. Everybody has it, everybody wants it. Is it a symptom of our throwaway days, or just another fad? Whatever the reason, nostalgia is fun – and a way of life, too, as Denis Gifford is consistently proving. His collection of kids' comics – the largest in England – is fast becoming a recognised source of social history, and with his carefully catalogued hoard of old movie stills, magazines, posters, and other faded ephemera, of all our yesterdays, forms the basis of more than one book. *Movie Monsters*, *Science Fiction Film*, *Discovering Comics*, *British Cinema*, *Stap Me – The British Newspaper Strip*, and *The Pictorial History of Horror Movies* are, says their busy author, just the start. You never can tell with NEL!

Also by Denis Gifford

BRITISH CINEMA
MOVIE MONSTERS
SCIENCE FICTION FILM
DISCOVERING COMICS
STAP ME! THE BRITISH NEWSPAPER STRIP.
THE PICTORIAL HISTORY OF HORROR MOVIES

Test Your N.Q.
(Nostalgia Quotient)

Devised and Compiled
by
Denis Gifford

NEW ENGLISH LIBRARY
TIMES MIRROR

For Pandy—another history book!

Many thanks to the Daily Mirror strip cartoon department, John Sanders of IPC Juveniles Division, and Keith MacKenzie of the Daily Mail, for the panels from strip cartoons reproduced in this book, which are the copyright of IPC Newspapers, IPC Publications, and Associated Newspapers.

An N.E.L. Original.

*

FIRST NEL PAPERBACK EDITION SEPTEMBER 1972

*

NEL Books are published by
New English Library Limited from Barnard's Inn, Holborn, London E.C.1.
Made and printed in Great Britain by Hunt Barnard Printing, Aylesbury, Bucks.

45001428 2

What's your N.Q.? and come to that, what's an N.Q.?

Do you O-lee-ay start-the-day right with 'Good morning! Nice day! I'll call again!'?

Do you open wide your window, dear, to see if the sun has got his hat on, and if he hasn't do you let a smile be your umbrella?

Did you Maclean your teeth today and then apply your shaving cream with a murmur of 'Not too little, not too much, but just right!'?

Do you say 'Ay thang yow!' to your bus conductor? Do you arrive at the office singing 'Hello again, I'm on the radio again'? When you knock-knock on the boss's door, and he calls out 'Who's there?', do you feel the urge to answer 'It's only me from over the sea'?

And when it's home from work you go ('Hi-ho hi-ho') and it's Monday Night at Eight O'Clock ('Oh can't you hear the chimes?'), do you sit and sigh for the days gone by with a heart-felt cry of 'Ee, if ever a man suffered'?

Then sigh no more, friend, for This Book is for You!

All that's wrong with you is a high N.Q. You just haven't been able to put it to use . . . until now. For N.Q. means Nostalgia Quotient, a hitherto neglected area of the human psyche. At last them days is gone for ever. Let this little book be your release from frustration, your key to happiness, and your passport to pleasure. What a Keyhole is to Kate, what a Cow Pie is to Desperate Dan, what Tea was to Our Ernie, this load of old rubbish can be to you!

Browse about in its heady if hairy pages; smile awhile at the merry memories it will stir up from your sludge; then show off to your chums with your newly-stimulated N.Q. glands all aglow. Like the old ad had it, 'Be the First in Your Neighbourhood' to have an N.Q. of 100. Or rather, 1,250! Be the Bob Monkhouse or the John Junkin of your radio set. Be the Phil Jenkinson or the Dick Vosburgh of your movie queue. Be the Ted Ray or the Arthur Askey of your Darby and Joan Club. Or cheat and be the Jack Watson or Denis Norden by mugging up the answers first – they are all packed at the back.

Yes, friends, no longer need you wait a week between *Sounds Familiar* shows on the radio (sorry – wireless) or between *Looks Familiar* shows on your telly. With this handy paperback you can have a touch of the old nostalgics *every* day!

Oh boy! I can hardly wait to read it – and I wrote it!

Denis Gifford

Introduction to Nostalgia

A few words from your chairman, Denis Norden

Nothing contributes more to the pleasure of Nostalgia than a bad memory. Except, possibly, Denis Gifford.

He's the man who devised a radio programme called *Sounds Familiar* and a TV programme called *Looks Familiar*. Both quizzes constitute a kind of University Of The Air course in Trivia, a measurement of Oh!-Level for the middle-aged.

The period Denis dwells on, drools over and wallows in stretches roughly from 1928 to 1948. A span of years peculiarly tender, painful and potent to many around today, myself included. (Frank Muir is an older generation completely.)

It was a time when the food we ate was thought out instead of thawed out. When the only film-stars who appeared without any clothes on were Lassie and Trigger. When you could light a cigarette from either end and people had children *after* they were married.

In those days, the only 'rock groups' to be found were working on Dartmoor, a 'demonstrator' was someone who sold novelty potato-peelers, and the only 'protest' song was 'I Won't Dance, Why Should I?'

All that 'up-tight' meant was being drunk in an aeroplane and Sex Education in schools was known as Playtime. 'Pot' was something you put a kid on, not tried to keep him off, and the biggest problem facing a parent was convincing his child that Dan Dare never bit *his* fingernails.

This was the period when beer had foam on it and washing-up water didn't. If you spent £5 at the grocers, you had trouble packing your purchases into the car boot. (Today, they'll fit in the glove-compartment.) The only 'swinger' was Tarzan, and if a girl were to come home and inform her parents she had hot pants, her mother made her take a cold bath. Radio was called 'the wireless', record-players were called 'gramophones' and a hair-dryer was a towel.

Isn't it different now! Radios don't have to be plugged in but toothbrushes do. We have wallpaper that won't show the dirt and cinemas that will. Gas-stoves are self-cleaning and teenagers aren't. Children who used to point a wooden pistol at you and say 'Bang-bang, you're dead!' now point a plastic tube and say 'Zap-zap, you're sterile!'.

Am I crying into my beer? Not really. The particular delight that Nostalgia bestows is difficult to pin down. I'm sure, though, that a large part of it is the realisation that things were not really as unbearably awful as they seemed at the time. To the extent that homesickness is a longing for the place you couldn't wait to get away from, much of middle-aged nostalgia is reminiscing about things you never actually did.

I'm all for it and so is Denis Gifford. I don't know about you. If you are of a generation that thinks Tom Mix is some kind of do-it-yourself cake-mixture – sorry, mate. There's nothing here for you. Go out and get some fresh air.

The rest of you – please join us. A wallow has been arranged.

Denis Norden

1: Start Part

For openers, what more appropriate than – openers? Everybody had one; from the Paramount mountain to the chimes of Big Ben, from the Gainsborough lady to the Luxembourg gong, from the six pips of Greenwich to the four poops of *Take It From Here*. Finding a good opener was half the hurdle; once Mrs Handley's boy (the original Mother's Pride and Joy) said 'Hello, soaks!' by chance, it got such a laugh it became a twenty year trade mark.

So what better way to open this Nostalgia Quiz book than by a quick canter through ten typical opening lines. Score one point for every comedian you can fit to these phrases.

1. GREETINGS, GENTLEFOLK!
2. GOOD ARTERNOON!
3. HOW DO – HOW ARE YER?
4. EVENIN' ALL!
5. GOOD EVENIN', CHUMS!
6. 'ALLO! 'ALLO! 'ALLO!
7. GOOD EVENING, ENGLAND!
8. AND A JOLLY GOOD EVENING TO ONE AND ALL!
9. WOTCHER COCKS!
10. HOWDY, FRIENDS AND NEIGHBOURS!

You'll find the answers in a special section at the back of the book. You'll find the answers to all the rest of the questions there, too, so no peeping!

The great stars of showbiz had another opening gambit to play, of course: the Signature Tune. To each his own, and as the boys in the pit, or Charlie Shadwell and the BBC Variety Orchestra, struck up the first few familiar bars, the audience would applaud loudly enough to drown the rest of the refrain. One point for every name you can pin to these signature songs of not so long ago.

11. SALLY
12. MARY FROM THE DAIRY
13. DAISY, DAISY
14. I LIFT UP MY FINGERS AND I SAY 'TWEET TWEET'
15. BIDDY MULLIGAN THE PRIDE OF THE COOMBE

16. STARDUST
17. THE PREPARATORY SCHOOL, THE PUBLIC SCHOOL, AND THE VARSITY
18. ONLY A ROSE
19. LOVE IN BLOOM
20. THE JOLLY BROTHERS

And for an extra Nostalgia Point: what was so special about the last signature tune?

But the best-remembered signature tunes, perhaps, are those that belonged to the bands. Dance bands, big bands, whatever you like to call them, each had its own distinctive style and its own distinctive sig. You win one point for every signature tune you can name for these five favourite bands.

21. JACK PAYNE
22. ROY FOX
23. BILLY COTTON
24. CARROLL GIBBONS
25. HENRY HALL

There's a catch in that one. It is cunningly worded to allow for six answers: six points.

Just so that this book can't be accused of British bias, here are five famous American bands: name their equally famous signature tunes.

26. CHARLIE BARNET
27. TOMMY DORSEY
28. ARTIE SHAW
29. GUY LOMBARDO
30. GLENN MILLER

Back to Britain; and who more British a bandleader than Geraldo ('On be'alf of me an' the boys, thanks fer list'nin'!'). He had a signature tune, of course, but an original one. Here is how it began, with all the 'boys' singing in a sawn-off stacatto. Join in and sing with me, then carry on where I leave off.

31. 'HELLO AGAIN, WE'RE ON THE RADIO AGAIN . . .'

Give yourself one point per line, up to a total of five!

2: Dance Chance

'Roll back the carpet, folks,' the compere would cry, 'Time for a programme of dance music!' I rolled back our carpet, folks – and found a tattered old copy of *Radio Times!* I still treasure it. So roll back your carpet, folks, and if you find one too, send it to me. I promise to pay you double the original market value: namely, fourpence!

Of course, the compere's original idea was slightly different. You were supposed to join in and dance to that swing, but I wonder how many listeners really did? I'm sure that like me, everybody simply sat back and smiled as a favourite dance band swung into the latest foxtrot or quickstep – or was it quicktrot and foxstep?

And it wasn't just the dances that had crazy names. Remember those bands? George Elrick and his Goofy Swing! Harry Bidgood and his Broadcasters! Noble Sissle and his Sizzling Syncopaters! Would you believe Gipsy Petulengro and his Lady Hussars?

Here are some British bands of those crazy days: one point for every band-leader you can fit to them.

1. .... AND HIS BANJOLIERS
2. .... AND HIS DUTCH SERENADERS
3. .... AND HIS COMMANDERS
4. .... AND HIS GLENEAGLES HOTEL BAND
5. .... AND HIS RKO-LIANS
6. .... AND HIS GAUCHO TANGO ORCHESTRA
7. .... AND HIS ROCKY MOUNTAIN RHYTHM
8. .... AND HIS TOWER BLACKPOOL BAND
9. .... AND HIS PICCADILLY HOTEL BAND
10. .... AND HIS SAVOY ORPHEANS

And just to prove that pre-war showbiz made its gesture towards Women's Lib, here are some female combinations – if you know what I mean.

11. .... AND HER ALL GIRLS' ORCHESTRA
12. .... AND HER WINNERS
13. .... AND HER STRICT TEMPO DANCE ORCHESTRA

The American bands were not to be outdone in the crazy quest for catchy combos. There now follows a hit parade of unlikely outfits: you fill in the front men.

14. .... AND HIS MOUND CITY BLUE BLOWERS
15. .... AND HIS CHARLESTON CHASERS
16. .... AND HIS CONNECTICUT YANKEES
17. .... AND HIS COLLEGIANS
18. .... AND HIS PIONEERS
19. .... AND HIS ISLANDERS
20. .... AND HIS TWELVE CLOUDS OF JOY

And now, for a change, we give you the names of the band-leaders. You add the bands for one point apiece. The bands listed above sound pretty funny today, but weren't supposed to at the time. The next bands were: supposed to sound funny, that is. And they often did.

21. SPIKE JONES AND HIS ....
22. SYD MILLWARD AND HIS ....
23. HARRY LESTER AND HIS ....
24. DOCTOR CROCK AND HIS ....
25. RED INGLE AND HIS ....
26. SYD SEYMOUR AND HIS ....
27. MICKEY KATZ AND HIS ....
28. FREDDIE MIRFIELD AND HIS ....

Finally, here is a whole host of band-leaders – but they are all fronting the wrong bands! One point for every combination you can correct.

29. HARRY PARRY AND HIS GROSVENOR HOUSE BAND
30. JOHNNY CLAES AND HIS RANCHERS
31. JOHNNY DENIS AND HIS GEORGIANS
32. SID LIPTON AND HIS COSTER PALS
33. LEON CORTEZ AND HIS CELESTE OCTET
34. FRANK BIFFO AND HIS CLAEPIGEONS
35. NAT GONELLA AND HIS BRASS QUINTET
36. J. H. SQUIRE AND HIS RADIO RHYTHM CLUB SEXTET
37. CIRO RIMAL AND HIS RUMBALAND MUCHACHOS

3: Name Game

What's in a name? To quote the immoral bird, roes by any other name would still smell. So much for heddification, as Professor Leon Cortez would have had it. And if you don't remember the Perfesser, then you have had it, too! At least, as far as your six bob goes. (And if you think I should have put that as 30p, then your N.Q.'s so low you'd better use this book as a crash course in history instead of as a quiz game!)

By their names shall ye know them: but by their *real* names do ye still know them? Once upon a time every film fan worth his salt (it came in little blue twists inside every bag of Smith's Crisps) knew the real names of his film favourites. How? It was the kind of secret the studios loved to share. Fan magazines like *Picture Show* and *Picturegoer* revealed such titbits of tittle-tattle in weekly dollops of useless information. The one dunned into my own dim recesses is 'Jack Oakie's real name is Lewis D. Offield. Wow!' Why they added 'Wow!' I'll never know. 'Ouch!', yes.

To open our Name Game here's a few for the film fans. Do you know the screen names of these famous stars of Hollywood? One point for each name you get right.

1. RUBY STEVENS
2. BILLIE CASSIN
3. GRETCHEN YOUNG
4. LUCILLE LANGHANKE
5. CONSTANCE KEANE

Now its the men's turn. Here come five top male stars, also from Hollywood's golden era. Score one point for each screen name you know belongs to:

6. FREDERICK BICKEL
7. ARCHIBALD LEACH
8. ARTHUR S. JEFFERSON
9. DANIEL KOMINSKY
10. REGINALD TRUSCOTT-JONES

Would they have attained the same fame had they kept the same name? There's no score for answering that one – but it's certainly a Talking Point (as *Picturegoer's* Lionel Collier would constantly claim). In fact, folks, if you use this Quiz Book as a party game (and why not), take time out from the question-answer routine to debate just such questions as that. We do it all the time on *Sounds Familiar* and *Looks Familiar*, and it can be a lot of fun. But back to the Name Game.

Talking of film stars and their real names, here comes a crop of pairs. Five couples who were often teamed together in the movies – but never like this!

11. FREDERICK AUSTERLITZ AND VIRGINIA MCMATH
12. JOSEPH YULE JR AND FRANCES GUMM
13. WILLIAM PRATT AND B. L. BLASKO
14. PHYLLIS BICKLE AND JAMES STEWART
15. LEONARD SLYE AND FRANCES BUTTS

(Yes, that *was* James Stewart – but it wasn't, if you see what I mean.) You score one point for each correct name, so there's a total of ten there. One of those film teams was British, by the way, if that's any help. Which leads us neatly into a short set of British film names. One point for each famous film star you can fit to these:

16. VIOLET PRETTY
17. GRETA WOXHOLT
18. MARGARET DAY
19. JUSTINE MCCARTHY
20. MAURICE MICKLEWHITE

Female film stars often change their names – by marrying. Yet they never change their screen names. If they did, their billing might read like the list that follows. If you can identify the lady stars, and their famous husbands, you score one point per name. Thus the next ten will get you twenty!

21. MURIEL FARR
22. DULCIE DENISON
23. HELEN HOWARD
24. KAY CLEMENTS
25. LILLI HARRISON
26. MARGARET HARVEY
27. VIRGINIA TRAVERS
28. JEAN GRANGER
29. JOAN NEWLEY
30. PATRICIA GREENE

Naturally, we don't guarantee that the ladies are still married to the gentlemen! But they were – once – and after all, this is the Nostalgia Game.

Of course, movies weren't always all-star affairs. There were lower case movies with film stars to match. Do you remember the 'B' pictures? Here are five stars of those minor movies, as they were at their baptisms. Can you guess the names they were best known by?

31. RICHARD VAN MATTIMORE
32. ROBERT HANKE
33. WARREN KNECH
34. MARY FREHSE
35. MARIE JURGENS

Now we'll go right back, back to the days of the silent screen. (Yes, I know its before your time, dear, but you can always pretend you're nostalgic for *Mad Movies!*) The game is the same: name the name of fame. One point for each still-famous star whose real name was:

36. DOUGLAS ULLMAN
37. JOHN BLYTHE
38. GLADYS SMITH
39. ERNEST CARLTON BRIMMER
40. APOLLONIA CHALUPEZ

Of course, these professional names are usually known as 'stage names', and that cues in a corner for all lovers of the legit. Our next list gives the real names of which famous stars of the stage?

41. GRACE STANSFIELD
42. GEORGE WADE
43. FANNY BORACH
44. RONALD HUTCHINSON
45. TOMMY SARGENT
46. ARTHUR MCEVOY
47. CARL PEDERSEN
48. HENRY LANE
49. ASA YOELSON
50. ALBERT POWELL

Next we present an all-star bill of comedians – or singers – or are they film stars? If you saw the following names posted outside your local theatre, what would you expect? Who would you expect? Are you sure? Take another look: there is something odd about each name; they all have something in common. There are two points available for each explanation.

51. JIMMY EDWARDS
52. TED RAY
53. JAMES MASON
54. ENGELBERT HUMPERDINCK
55. HENRY HALL
56. JIMMY RODGERS

If you haven't spotted the link and have got this far, then here is a clue: 'The name's the same!' Now you score only one point apiece: a total of six instead of twelve. Even less marks come your way for this last Name Game:

57. LON CHANEY, TOM WALLS, GEORGE FORMBY, CARL LAEMMLE, WILL HAY, MARIE LLOYD, EFREM ZIMBALIST.

For one point, what have they got in common?

4: Initial Entry

It sounds as if this quiz should have come first in the book, but in fact our Initial Entry in the Name Game requires you to do exactly that: enter the initials! You'd be surprised how many famous people in showbiz are known by their initials. Here are half a dozen, each without their customary initial. One point for each one you ink in correctly.

1. .... CARROL NAISH
2. .... AUBREY SMITH
3. .... ARTHUR RANK
4. .... SYLVAN SIMON
5. .... DEMPSEY TABLER
6. .... EYNON EVANS

Now we move down one: this time the missing initials come mid-way through the signatures.

7. JOE .... BROWN
8. CHARLES .... COCHRAN
9. SAMUEL .... HINDS
10. ANNA .... NILLSON
11. CECIL .... DE MILLE
12. JACK .... LEONARD

Part three: personalities who are known by their initials alone. Two initials apiece, and therefore two marks, too.

13. .... CLIVE
14. .... STEVENS
15. .... PULLY
16. .... DEVLIN
17. .... WHITEHEAD
18. .... PROBY

.... *Proby??* (Well, we've got to throw one in for the kids now and then!).

Sounds Familiar is the radio version of this game, so it's high time we tuned in our catswhiskers and crystals. Here come five famous personalities of the radio (sorry, wireless), each of whom was better known by their initials than by their Christian names.

19. .... GRISEWOOD
20. .... MIDDLETON
21. .... CAMPBELL
22. .... EMMETT
23. .... BARRINGTON-DALBY

With one point possible for each correctly entered initial, you can notch up a neat ten there (thanks to a bit of luck with numbers 22 and 23!)

5: Mister Twister

No names, no pack drill – but six points for you if you can name the actors who played these nearly nameless ones of the wireless. And one extra point apiece if you can also name the radio series from which they sprang. Thus a total of twelve.

1. MR MUDDLECOMBE
2. MR TRUMBLE
3. MR GROWSER
4. MR FOX
5. MR WIMPLE
6. MR PASTRY

'This is the missis' once went a song, and there will be misses for you if you fail to score one point apiece for naming the actresses who played these missuses of the wirelesses. Again, there is an extra point for each of the radio series they appeared in, giving a total of twelve.

7. MRS MOP
8. MRS BUGGINS
9. MRS BAGWASH
10. MRS TICKLE
11. MRS HOSKINS
12. MRS SHUFFLEWICK

6: Bracket Racket

For a host of showbiz stars, the issue Christian name and surname was never enough. They had to add a middle name and, what's more, add it in brackets. This set a problem for title designers and poster painters, and it now sets one for you. Here are some American film stars with their middles missing. One point for every correct name you fill in the empty brackets.

1. GEORGE ( ) HAYES
2. AL ( ) ST. JOHN
3. HENRY ( ) MORGAN
4. GUINN ( ) WILLIAMS
5. WILLIAM ( ) PHIPPS
6. WALTER ( ) PALANCE
7. ELROY ( ) HIRSCH

British stars got into the bracket racket, too. One point for each name missing from the following brackets.

8. JACK ( ) WATSON
9. JOE ( ) HENDERSON
10. JACKIE ( ) HUNTER
11. HERSCHEL ( ) HENLERE
12. RICHARD ( ) MURDOCH
13. BILLY ( ) SCOTT

Just so that we don't end on an unlucky number, one more name from the American music scene.

14. JOE ( ) CARR

7: Middle Riddle

For some folks, two names are never enough: to be heard they need a third. Certainly the following line-up looks odd without the customary middle bits. You score a point for every missing middle name you can name.

1. HOWARD CRAWFORD
2. ENID TAYLOR
3. DAVID SMITH
4. JOHN DAVIES
5. EDNA OLIVER
6. ANTHONY ALLAN
7. LILIAN DAVIS
8. WILFRID WHITE
9. BRIAN HURST
10. PETER HILL

8: None Fun

Or the No Name Game. A handful of stars became known, not by their names, but by their descriptions. Do you recall whom once they called:

1. THE VOICE
2. THE LOOK
3. THE THREAT
4. THE BACK
5. THE BODY

9: Same Name

A game of 'The Name's the Same' again – but with a twist. Can you name the showbiz personalities whose names fit the following? One surname – but two points – for each.

1. A BOXER AND A BROTHER
2. A HILLBILLY AND A SOUP
3. A SINGING FAMILY AND A LIVER PILL
4. A COMEDIAN AND A MONASTERY
5. A FAMILY AND A CORNER HOUSE
6. A SISTER AND A SALT
7. MAID MARIAN AND AN AIRPLANE
8. A GANGSTER AND A BARLEY WATER
9. A HIP-FLASK AND A TOILET
10. DR JEKYLL AND MR SOUSA

10: Nick Trick

'They call them Yanks, my lord!' There's a touch of the old nostalgia for you. Remember that regular feature of the old *London Opinion* magazine? Just a bonus glow by way of intro to a quick quiz on musicians of the jazz and swing era: Americans, of course. Many of them were known by their nicknames alone: real names were never divulged, except on reissue record sleeves. Here's a list of internationally-known nicknames. One point for every correct surname you add.

1. KING
2. DUKE
3. COUNT
4. EARL
5. LORD
6. LADY
7. POPS
8. FATHA
9. SONNY
10. KID
11. BABY
12. THE MAN

All right, all right, so some of them weren't nicknames. But it seemed a shame to spoil the family tree. The names that follow are definitely of the old nick. If they are not then somebody's vicar must have got a shock!

13. SATCHELMOUTH
14. JELLYROLL
15. LEADBELLY
16. WOODY
17. WINGY
18. MUGGSY
19. BUDDY
20. PEANUTS
21. BUNK
22. HOT LIPS
23. ZIGGY
24. ZUTTY

In good nick are the musical stars who labour under these labels. All the nicknames are relevant to size and shape.

25. FATS
26. SLIM
27. TUBBY
28. SKINNY
29. SHORTY

11: Wrong Song

Here's a who's who of top pops from the past, but this quiz is a case of 'the singer not the song' – for this list has missed by a twist. Can you correct the line-up by placing the right song against the right singer? If it helps at all, they are all Americans.

1. FRED ASTAIRE	IT'S MAGIC
2. TERESA BREWER	MY FOOLISH HEART
3. BING CROSBY	ANY TIME
4. DORIS DAY	THE DONKEY SERENADE
5. BILLY ECKSTINE	THAT'S WHAT I LIKE ABOUT THE SOUTH
6. EDDIE FISHER	THE RIDDLE SONG
7. JUDY GARLAND	MULE TRAIN
8. PHIL HARRIS	HORSES DON'T BET ON PEOPLE
9. BURL IVES	HOW MUCH IS THAT DOG IN THE WINDOW
10. ALLAN JONES	THE LITTLE WHITE CLOUD THAT CRIED
11. KAY KYSER	COW COW BOOGIE
12. FRANKIE LAINE	SIX LESSONS FROM MADAME LAZONGA
13. ELLA MAY MORSE	G'BYE NOW
14. GERTRUDE NEISEN	TESS'S TORCH SONG
15. HELEN O'CONNELL	MY VERY GOOD FRIEND THE MILKMAN
16. PATTI PAGE	PENNIES FROM HEAVEN
17. JOHNNIE RAY	THE WHIFFENPOOF SONG
18. DINAH SHORE	I WANNA GET MARRIED
19. MARTHA TILTON	MUSIC, MUSIC, MUSIC
20. RUDY VALLEE	TOP HAT
21. FATS WALLER	OVER THE RAINBOW

Okay, all you British Rubbish Collectors, now its our turn. Do the same thing again: line up the singers with their songs.

22. LES ALLEN	LITTLE OLD LADY
23. AL BOWLLY	ANSWER ME
24. DOROTHY CARLESS	TO EACH HIS OWN
25. BERYL DAVIS	IN A SHADY NOOK
26. RAY ELLINGTON	THE GIPSY
27. GRACIE FIELDS	ROOM 504
28. CARROLL GIBBONS	LITTLE MAN YOU'VE HAD A BUSY DAY
29. LESLIE HUTCHINSON	SO DEEP IS THE NIGHT
30. DICK JAMES	BEER BARREL POLKA
31. KATHIE KAYE	CLIMB UP THE WALL
32. VERA LYNN	ROBIN HOOD
33. SCOTTY MCHARG	THESE FOOLISH THINGS
34. JESSIE MATTHEWS	THE BELLS OF ST MARY'S
35. MONTY NORMAN	AUF WIEDERSEHEN MY DEAR
36. DONALD PEERS	OVER MY SHOULDER
37. MONTE REY	THE THREE BEARS
38. DOROTHY SQUIRES	MY HEART GOES CRAZY
39. BRUCE TRENT	COMES LOVE
40. BERTHA WILLMOTT	WE'LL MEET AGAIN
41. YANA	JIMMY UNKNOWN

12: Number Lumber

'And our next number is a snappy little one', announced the band-leader all unwittingly. A surprising number of numbers have been written about numbers. Can you insert the missing numbers in the following numbers? Number one point for every number you number correctly.

1. GIVE ME ... MINUTES MORE
2. GIVE ME ... ROSES
3. THE ... I LOVE
4. ... LITTLE SISTERS
5. I'M ... TODAY
6. ... MORE MONTHS AND ... MORE DAYS
7. ... LONELY DAYS MAKE ONE LONELY WEEK
8. ... LESSONS FROM MADAME LA ZONGA
9. YOU CAN'T MARRY ... PRETTY GIRLS
10. ... FEVVERS ON A FRUSH

From actual numbers to the more expected kind of number. Here are some clues to famous song numbers of yesterday. Can you answer the questions correctly? Here's an example:

Q: WHO STOLE MY HEART AWAY?
A: NO-ONE BUT YOU!

Got it? Okay – let's see how you do with these. The usual one point per correct answer.

11. WHERE DOES IT LOOK LIKE RAIN?
12. WHAT MORE CAN I SAY?
13. WHY MUST IT BE JELLY?
14. WHO'S THAT KNOCKING AT THE DOOR?
15. I'D SWAP MY HORSE AND DOG FOR WHO?
16. WHOSE IS THE FACE IN THE MISTY NIGHT?
17. NO-ONE COULD EVER REPLACE WHO?
18. WHY HAS A COW GOT FOUR LEGS?
19. WHEN YOU HEAR THE WHISTLE BLOWING EIGHT TO THE BAR THEN YOU KNOW WHAT?
20. WHO'S GOING TO MEND THE WHISTLE?

No dance band programme would have been considered complete without its medley, a melange of popular songs strung together by some tenuous link. Here is our N.Q. medley, ten tunes each with a colour in the title.

21. THAT OLD ... MAGIC
22. ... CHAMPAGNE
23. ... EYES
24. THE ... ROSE OF TEXAS
25. DEEP ...
26. ... CHRISTMAS
27. ... RIBBONS
28. THE OLD ... FLUTE
29. THE LADY IN ...
30. THE ... DANUBE

13: Absurd Word

Singalong time again, folks. Welcome to 'They don't write songs like they used to' Department. Will you agree with that old saw when you remember the lines immediately following those quoted below? One point for each line you remember, and an extra Nostalgia Point if you sing them out good and loud, wherever you may be! You deserve it!

1. CHICKERY CHICK CHA-LA-CHA-LA . . .
2. MAIRZY DOATS AND DOAZY DOATS . . .
3. HOLD TIGHT, HOLD TIGHT, HOLD TIGHT, HOLD TIGHT . . .
4. BOOP BOOP DITTEM . . .
5. CEMENT MIXER . . .

14: Keyboard Chord

'They laughed when I sat down at the piano': So ran a famous pre-war ad. 'They'd taken the stool away!' So ran an equally famous pre-war gag. But nobody laughed when these ten famous stars sat down at the piano – although they might have if their billing had read as follows.

1. CHARLIE CAVALLARO
2. CARROLL CAVENDISH
3. KAY KUNZ
4. ARTHUR AUGUST
5. PATRICIA YOUNG
6. RONALD MAYERL
7. BILLY ROSSBOROUGH
8. JAN LOWRY
9. CARMEN GIBBONS
10. TONY GOURLAY

Yes, we've mucked them all up again! One point for each name you can straighten out.

Where one piano wasn't noise enough, only two would do. The double act at double pianos was a great favourite with audiences whose eardrums were as yet unpierced by air raid sirens. Here are five famous two-piano acts, but each has the wrong partner. Sort them out for a point apiece.

11. RAWICZ AND DORIS ARNOLD
12. REUB SILVER AND DAVE KAYE
13. HARRY S. PEPPER AND MARION DAY
14. JOSE AND LANDAUER
15. IVOR MORETON AND AMPARO ITURBI

One more mixup before we leave the keyboard. This time the spotlight is on those maestros of the mighty Wurlitzers, the prewar kings of the ice-cream intervals, the cinema organists. One point and a Flavour of the Month for every organist you unscramble.

16. TERENCE TORCH
17. REGINALD RICHMOND
18. SANDY MACLEAN
19. ROBINSON PAGAN
20. ROBIN DE JONG
21. BOBBY DIXON
22. FLORENCE FOORT
23. SIDNEY CASEY
24. QUENTIN CLEAVER
25. REGINALD MACPHERSON

By way of a quickie before we go, and bearing in mind the subject of this section, which of the following stars is the Odd Man Out?

26. ARTHUR ASKEY
DON BRADMAN
FRED EMNEY
YVONNE ARNAUD
BILLY BENNETT
REG VARNEY

15: Double Trouble

Double your pleasure, double your fun: so runs the modern rune according to Wrigley. In the pre-telly days of Saturday Night Music Hall, producer John Sharman doubled our pleasure and doubled our fun by booking double acts. The only thing he didn't double was the pay cheque! The formula was always the same: one straight man, one comic. And it is the same today, for the double act is still a staple of showbiz, and will remain so as long as Morecambe is Wise enough to stick with it. One point for each of the following classic comedy couples you can complete, and no points for that horrible pun cracked one sentence back.

1. MURRAY AND ....
2. BENNETT AND ....
3. WHEELER AND ....
4. CLAPHAM AND ....
5. COLLINSON AND ....

If you are really hot on your old-time comedy, you will be able to score two points on that last pair. Collinson had two team-mates in his time, and what's more they make a rhyme! There's help!

The next group of double acts sound so familiar that to score you have to remember their Christian names, which don't. Six names, six points.

6. FLANAGAN AND ALLEN
7. NERVO AND KNOX
8. NAUGHTON AND GOLD

And for an easy Nostalgia Point,

9. WHAT HAVE THEY GOT IN COMMON?

The following line-up of double acts also have something in common, but your main job is to name the leading comedian in each partnership.

10. .... AND BILLIE CARLISLE
11. .... AND ENID TREVOR
12. .... AND HILDA MUNDY
13. .... AND BOBBIE
14. .... AND ELSIE DAY

Now that you've done them, it should be an easy Nostalgia point for you to say

15. WHAT HAVE THEY GOT IN COMMON?

Double acts, double names, and double points coming up. Here are five partnerships that weren't! That is to say, they were on the wireless every week, yet didn't exist! To put it another way, these fellows were phoney – pseudonymous performers. These non-names concealed ten totally unrelated comedians who teamed up from time to time as double acts, just for the radio. So there are ten points for you if you can name the names behind the names.

16. MURGATROYD AND WINTERBOTTOM
17. ALEXANDER AND MOSE
18. FLOTSAM AND JETSAM
19. MAJOR AND MINOR
20. BLACK AND BLEW

If you have an exceptionally high N.Q. you will have an alternative name in mind for one of the acts. If so, and you're right, award yourself a bonus Nostalgia Point.

16: Three Spree

Three-handed acts are less frequently found: perhaps it's true that three's a crowd. Here are just three threesomes, and thus three points if you can add the missing name to each.

1. FORSYTH, SEAMON AND ....
2. VINE, MORE AND ....
3. THE ORGAN, THE DANCEBAND AND ....

17: Fame Game

From time to time, out of the close harmony of a group, there emerged a singer who became a star in his or her own right. Can you name

1. ONE FAMOUS ANDREWS SISTER
2. ONE FAMOUS INK SPOT
3. ONE FAMOUS RHYTHM BOY
4. ONE FAMOUS BOSWELL SISTER
5. ONE FAMOUS STOOGE

18: Team Scream

Double acts and other partnerships are often billed by surnames alone, yet everybody knows their Christian names. Or do they? Do you? Here are ten partnerships billed by their first names alone. You name their surnames. The first is easy, the rest – well, that depends on your N.Q.

1. STAN AND OLLIE
2. BING AND BOB
3. BOB AND DENIS
4. FRANK AND DENIS
5. BERT AND BOB
6. BUD AND LOU
7. KENNETH AND GEORGE
8. DEAN AND JERRY
9. HARRY AND VICTOR
10. ELSIE AND DORIS

Real double trouble this time – the acts are all mixed up. Straighten them out into their correct pairs for one point apiece.

11. FRANK AND EDGAR
12. AMOS AND ERNEST
13. LUCAN AND MCCARTHY
14. REVNELL AND WILLIAMS
15. MORECAMBE AND WEST
16. HAVER AND ANDY
17. STANELLI AND MACSHANE
18. NONI AND LEE
19. BENNETT AND WISE
20. BERGEN AND PARTNER

A few famous teams played as 'characters' – in other words, they called themselves by different names while performing their skits. Who were

21. CUTHBERT AND PUSSYFOOT
22. DUCKHEAD AND EGGBLOW
23. MICK AND MONTMORENCY
24. GERT AND DAISY

19: West Test

Saddle up your mustangs, lasso your stetsons, hitch up your stirrups, and bust your broncos, pardners, for hyar's whar we hit the trail to the old Bar-NQ fer a roundup of western questerns. The West that Never Was has always played a big part in the showbiz scene, even though, as the song once sang, 'Them Hillbillies is Mountain Williams now!' First off, here's a posse of movie cowboys caught short without their horses. One point for every four-legged friend you can name for:

1. ROY ROGERS
2. GENE AUTRY
3. KEN MAYNARD
4. TEX RITTER
5. TOM MIX
6. ALLAN LANE

Your cowboy hero had a two-legged friend, too. He was known in the trade as the Comical Sidekick, which didn't mean he laughed when you kicked him in the side! He was the hero's buddy, who stuck to the star through thick and thin: which is a fair description of the sizes of their respective wage packets. Here are the stars: one point for every Comical Sidekick you can remember.

7. WILLIAM BOYD
8. ROY ROGERS
9. GENE AUTRY
10. TEX RITTER
11. JOHNNY MACK BROWN
12. DUNCAN RENALDO
13. TIM HOLT
14. LASH LARUE
15. RAY 'CRASH' CORRIGAN

One famous fictional character of western movies had a horse and a sidekick. He was known as 'The Lone Ranger' and was played by several actors. For one point each, name

16. THE LONE RANGER'S HORSE
17. THE LONE RANGER'S SIDEKICK

It was easy to spot the baddies in the 'B' westerns: they were the ones in the black hats with moustaches to match. They were also played by the same actors every time. Here is the repertory company of 'B' baddies, but being baddies they are trying to hide under aliases. One point for each Christian name you correctly align with a surname.

18. ROY LONDON
19. I. STANFORD BARCROFT
20. TOM DUNCAN
21. KENNE KING
22. GEORGE JOLLEY
23. MORRIS COFFIN
24. CHARLES CHESEBRO
25. TRISTRAM ANKRUM

'B' western titles are the most forgettable in Hollywood history. There was really only one title which was continually permutated. To prove our point, here are ten titles all of which sound familiar, none of which exist. They are mixed up in the same way as our crazy mixed-up villains. One point for each title you can sort out correctly.

26. BELLS OF THE GOLDEN WEST
27. YODELIN' KID FROM THE GOLDEN WEST
28. HOME IN PINE RIDGE
29. MAN FROM MEXICO WAY
30. SPRINGTIME IN WYOMIN'
31. HEART OF THE ROCKIES
32. IN OLD MONTANA SKIES
33. PALS OF CALIENTE
34. DOWN SAN ANGELO
35. BLUE MUSIC MOUNTAIN

Many of the stars of 'B' class westerns had, it seems, no Christian names. They were known, not by their brands, but by their handles: nicknames. One point for every correct surname you hitch onto the following nicknames.

36. WHIP
37. FUZZY
38. GABBY
39. BUCK
40. HOOT
41. WILD BILL
42. RED

43. ROCKY
44. BUSTER
45. SUNSET

Although silent movies had long since faded into the sunset, 'B' Westerns still had subtitles. These were the catchlines, often in brackets, that the publicity departments of Columbia and Republic appended to the names of their stars, and even their stars' horses. One point for each name you can fit to the following film phrases.

46. THE KING OF THE COWBOYS
47. THE SMARTEST HORSE IN THE MOVIES
48. THE SINGING COWBOY
49. THE WONDER HORSE
50. THE ARIZONA COWBOY
51. THE KING OF THE WILD WEST
52. THE QUEEN OF THE WEST

One brand-mark of the B-movie was that once every reel the plot stopped for a song. Usually it was the star who pulled out his guitar and twanged a tune or two. Just as frequently, the cowhands would gather round the old camp fire and, surprise surprise, turn out to be that well-loved signing team, Chuck Wagon and the Cayuses. Here are several such singing teams from western movies, only their names have been scrambled. Sort them out for one point apiece.

53. LULUBELLE AND ELVIRY
54. BOB WILLING AND THE RIDERS OF THE PIONEERS
55. THE HOOSIER BROTHERS AND SCOTTY
56. WEAVER AND THE SONS OF THE PURPLE SAGE
57. FOY NOLAN AND THE HOTSHOTS

20: Strip Trip (No. 1)

When you were a kid, what did you buy with your Saturday penny? My mates bought chips, but I bought *Chips*: eight pink pages packed with prime pow for a paltry penny! Fun galore to make you roar, as the editor was wont to put it, and as like as not a Grand Free Gift to boot. What days we had, and what daze the characters had, as they slapsticked their slap-happy way through panel after panel of 'oops' and 'eeks', 'ouches' and 'eeshes'!

Through the courtesy of IPC Juveniles Division, who now hold the rights in many of those old bygone delights, the NQ Book proudly presents a parade of those alltime, oldtime old-timers. How many of them do you remember?

1. Our premier panel pictures a pair known far and wide as 'The World Famous Tramps'. They copped the copper on the front page of which comic? An extra point if you remember the *full* title of the comic.

2. Two more tramps, believe it or not, despite the tip-top topper and the high-class eye-glass. These two were noted for their 'World-Wide Wanderings'. Which comic did they star in and, for an extra Nostalgic Point, what was the colour of the paper it was printed on?

3. The double act was standard stuff in the comic papers of old. Here the double act is doubled, and so are your points if you can name the two heroes thundering over the horizon to put paid to the regular deviltry of – who? Two more points for the names of the villains; and one more for the name of the comic they all appeared in.

1

WINDOW CLEANING CO

2

RESERVED FOR THE 1ST MATE
RESERVED FOR CAPT. RAVENROAR

3

VOT HO! HERE IT VOS!
SECRET

Here are three more nostalgic nudges from the pre-war penny comics.

4. Tramps and layabouts didn't have things all their own way in the comics. Not when this comical constabule was about. Name him, name his comic (he starred on the front page for years), and for a third Nostalgia Point, name his superior (in rank only), the Inspector.

5. Two lady coppers now: let nobody say the pre-war comics were anti-Women's Lib! You'll never remember the name of the officer in the cap – it was Clara – but surely you could never forget the pretty one in the helmet, the curls, and the legs? Another point if you name her comic.

6. Coppers again, cadets this time. They were known as 'The Kid Cops' – but what were their names? If it helps, they never seemed to possess surnames. The name of the comic they patrolled (on page five) will cop you an extra point.

4

5

6

This time our subject is the services.

7. The senior service first, of course, and first for fun, right on page one, were these super sailors. A clue: the names of the same make the name of a game. Score an extra point for the name of the comic; if it helps the penguin was called Pengy!

8. All up in the air is our next comic character. He roared about on the front page of a famous comic printed on green paper; and the readers roared about, too. He wasn't strictly a service man, being closer kin to the layabouts depicted on page one of our comic section. One extra Nostalgia Point for the name of his dog, who more usually acted as the rudder!

9. Bringing up the rear, here comes the British Army, in the shape of a couple of comical cadets. Their subtitle was 'The Boys of the Bold Brigade', and they caused a weekly riot in the pages of – what? It was usually a blue comic, occasionally white, sometimes yellow! Your extra Nostalgia Point comes if you can identify the Sergeant seen somewhat stunned in the background.

7

PLAY!

8

GOT YOU MISTER BIG BULLY!

9

WE'VE COME OUT ON THE RIGHT SIDE AFTER ALL! TUCK AWAY, CHUMMY!

Our next selection from yesteryear comprises three scenes from family life.

10. Here is a dad and his lad who appeared top right in the centre spread of which comic? It was on pink paper, and their names all began with P.

11. From a dad and his lad to a mum and her chum. Possibly a widow, more likely an abandoned woman (if you see what I mean), this horrendous harridan and her halfwit halfpint ran regularly in a blue paper comic which turned white when the war came. (Didn't we all!)

12. Back to the healthy father-and-son relationship with a vengeance! This pair pranked peculiarly upon page one of a popular penn'orth in the pre-war period. (No, their names didn't begin with a P; whatever gave you that idea?) Name them, and their comic: one point apiece.

10

JUST THINK OF THE SPORT WE CAN HAVE CATCHING THESE FISH AND THROWING 'EM BACK AGAIN

11

OW! MA'S COLLARED ME!
I CAN'T SLAP MRS. STINGY, BUT I CAN YOU. COME HERE!

12

CINEMA

Opposite we find more kids at their comical cut-ups. This time they are all schoolboys.

13. The two little chums who grace the right-hand side of the picture were bosom buddies back in the days when there was no colour bar in the comics: except where printer's ink was concerned. This comic was not published in colour, although its paper was: green. There are two points here: one for the kids' names, one for the name of their comic. And for a third Nostalgia Point, what was the name of their school?

14. Here's another kid who caused trouble for his teacher. His comic was green, but he wasn't; nor, incidentally, was it the same comic as the one mentioned in Question 13 above. His hat should give you a clue, and as an extra hint, he was subtitled: 'He's Not So Silly As He Looks!' Three points: one for his name, one for his comic, and your Nostalgia Point for the name of his teacher.

15. Aha! (Or do we mean, Yarooh!) Here's one you're bound to get. You even get a name clue in the picture. This happy family reunion, a rare sight, shows 'The Fattest Schoolboy On Earth' (as he was subtitled, with Pa, Ma, sis and brother. Lots of points here: One for our hero, one for his sister's name, one for his school, one for the paper he first appeared in, and one for the comic from which this scene was snipped. Extra Nostalgia Point: the name of his creator. Extra extra Nostalgia Point: the *real* name of his creator!

13

HA! HA! HE'S GONE IN OFF DE DEEP END!

14

CRACK!

15

HALLO DAD!"
SAMMY!
HALLO, MUM! WHERE'S THE GRUB?

The last page of our comic section (Shame!) for the present (Hooray!). Four miscellaneous pictures from four miscellaneous characters, which we shall entitle, Miscellaneous.

16. Here's a comical crew of characters from a favourite comic. The hero is on the floor, as usual, and the villains have won the plans and the day. Name our hero, the king, the glamorous 'Gal Pal', and the villain: his full name, not just the matey abbreviation given in the rhyming balloon. A clue: our hero was subtitled 'The Ancient Brit', and you should be able to name the comic because it was recently revived.

17. Here's the hero of a war-time comic paper, stretching a point, and his arm, in the pursuit of rough justice. What was his name, and descriptive subtitle. If it helps, they rhymed. Extra point for the name of the comic.

18. Animal heroes are rare in British comics, but these two cute customers ran for nigh on fifty years in the same comic. What were their names (one point apiece), and the name of the comic (another point).

19. A classic closeup as a grand finale to our comic section. Who's the halfpint hero getting his ears scrubbed by his Ma? Clue, Ma had her full name in the lad's subtitle. A point for the lad, another for his comic, and an extra Nostalgia Point for the name of his pet caterpillar, getting it in the eye lower left.

And so we close our comic section, chums! But dry your damp peepers, there's more fun to come!

16

IT'S WHIZZY! HE'S SNAFFLED MY PLANS AND I'M BAFFLED!

17
18

19

21: Phrase Daze

In the golden days of radio you wouldn't catch a comedian without his catch-phrase, that ever-ready way to raise a laugh. *Itma* critics (oh yes, there were a few!) said if you took away Tommy Handley's catchphrases his half-hour show would only run five minutes! So taking *Itma* for starters, try to name the characters who laid claim to these immortal sayings. Characters' names only, mind; we're saving the actors who played them for another quiz! Meanwhile, you can win one point apiece.

1. 'CAN I DO YER NOW, SIR?'
2. 'EVERY PENNY MAKES THE WATER WARMER!'
3. 'BOSS, BOSS, SUMP'N TERRIBLE'S HAPPENED!'
4. 'NOTHING AT ALL, NOTHING AT ALL!'
5. 'IT'S BEIN' SO CHEERFUL AS KEEPS ME GOIN'!'
6. 'MISTER HAND-LAY!!'
7. 'MY PAPA HE SAY . . .'
8. 'AFTER YOU, CLAUDE!'
9. 'I DON'T MIND IF I DO!'
10. 'GOOD MORNING! NICE DAY!'

Our next batch of instant ha-ha's comes from one single show, too. This time we aren't telling you which – you get one extra point for knowing that.

11. 'RESERVOIR OLD DEAR AND BOB'S YER FLIPPIN' UNCLE!'
12. 'NYEDEN, NYADEN, NYEDEN, NEGGITY CROP DE BOMBIT!'
13. 'HUSH! KEEP IT DARK!'
14. 'OH, I SAY, I RATHER CARE FOR THAT!'
15. 'CARRY ON SMOKIN'!'
16. 'SOMEBODY CA-ALL?'

And the name of the show was

17. WHAT?

It wasn't just characters in the radio series that had catch-phrases, comedians had them too. See if you can remember who said the following Famous Laugh Words.

18. 'MIND MY BIKE!'
19. 'AY THANG YOW!'
20. 'I'VE ONLY GOT FOUR MINUTES!'
21. 'HOW'S YOUR FATHER?'
22. 'PIN BACK YOUR LUG'OLES.'
23. 'WHAT'S-A MATTER WIT'CHEW?'
24. 'HAVE YOU READ ANY GOOD BOOKS LATELY?'
25. 'AS LONG AS WE KNOW IT'LL BE QUITE ALL RIGHT!'
26. 'GERROFF ME FOOT!'
27. 'YOU SHOULD USE STRONGER ELASTIC!'
28. 'FLIPPIN' KIDS!'
29. 'NOW, ER, LADIES AND GENTLEMEN!'
30. 'YOU LUCKY PEOPLE!'

Back to the characters again, and this time we operate a double points score system. First you name the character, then you name the radio series.

31. 'HE'S LOVELY, MRS HOSKINS, HE'S LOOOVELY!'
32. 'MIGHTY FINE!'
33. 'GOOD MORNIN' SIR, WAS THERE SOMETHING?'
34. 'WOTCHER TISH!'
35. 'ARGY-BARGY! ARGY-BARGY!'
36. 'IT'S DISGRRRRACEFUL!'
37. 'VERY TASTY – VERY SWEET!'
38. 'ONE NIGHT AS I WAS SITTING ROUND ME OLD FIRE BUCKET ...'
39. 'DOWN IN THE JUNGLE CHANTING EVERY DAY ...'
40. 'COME 'OME, JIM EDWARDS.'
41. 'REE-DICULOUS!!'
42. 'I'VE ARRIVED AND TO PROVE IT I'M 'ERE!'

22: Song Throng

Time for music again, and here is a hit parade of top pops from the days before there were such things. Had there been, then these titles would have been bang at the head of the lists. Each of these top songs had its top singer, the one we went for on the record label. One point for each singer you can remember.

1. AIN'T IT GRAND TO BE BLOOMING WELL DEAD
2. SHE'S MY LOVELY
3. THE LAMBETH WALK
4. LEAVE THE PRETTY GIRLS ALONE
5. GOODBYE SALLY
6. GOODNIGHT VIENNA
7. LOUISE
8. I DON'T WANT TO GO TO BED
9. THE MUSIC GOES ROUND AND AROUND
10. YOU TOO CAN BE THE LIFE OF THE PARTY

As a rather belated clue, all the singers were men. So if you have to go back and change anything, you lose half a point for each alteration!

Now it's the ladies' turn. The next songs were sung by female women of the opposite sex (bonus Nostalgia Point for the name of the comedian who cracked that!). (11)

12. NO! NO! A THOUSAND TIMES NO!
13. THE SAILOR WITH THE NAVY BLUE EYES
14. THERE'S SOMETHING ABOUT A SOLDIER
15. ONLY A GLASS OF CHAMPAGNE
16. ME AND MY DOG ARE LOST IN A FOG

Only the lady sang it, 'Me and my dorg are lorst in the forg!' Does that help? If it does, lop off half a mark. The one star/one song formula spans right back to the days of the Music Halls, of course. Here are ten of the best-remembered Music Hall songs: but are their singers best-remembered, too? You score one point for every star you can recall who sang:

17. WHEN FATHER PAPERED THE PARLOUR
18. I USED TO SIGH FOR THE SILVERY MOON
19. ON MOTHER KELLY'S DOORSTEP
20. LEANING ON A LAMP-POST
21. THE END OF THE ROAD
22. I BELONG TO GLASGOW
23. BOILED BEEF AND CARROTS
24. TWO LOVELY BLACK EYES
25. I STOPPED, I LOOKED, AND I LISTENED
26. THE LAUGHING POLICEMAN

And those ten were all men! Any hasty alterations lose you a half a point per. Now the girls can have a go.

27. JUST LIKE THE IVY
28. WAITING AT THE CHURCH
29. BURLINGTON BERTIE FROM BOW
30. ALL THE NICE GIRLS LOVE A SAILOR
31. DON'T HAVE ANY MORE MRS MOORE
32. SHE'S A LASSIE FROM LANCASHIRE
33. MY MOTHER SAID ALWAYS LOOK UNDER THE BED
34. MY OLD MAN SAID FOLLOW THE VAN
35. JOSHUA

23: Who's Who

Once upon a night-time the air was alive with the sounds of laughter. These were the real funnymen of radio, not the solo stars but the supporting players, the character voices, the ho-ho host of multi-toned merrymakers who now people our past with faceless phrases. Their creations were real to us, but existed only in our mind's eyes. We clothed their voices with faces of our own fancy.

Here are some of the great radio characters: can you name the people who played them (for one point) and the shows they appeared in (for another).

1. OLD EBENEZER
2. MR WALKER
3. MR WHATSISNAME
4. FARMER WILL WATCHET
5. PEEP KEYHOLE
6. EDIE ARUNDEL
7. GEORGE FILTH
8. ENOCH
9. GRIMBLE
10. RON GLUM
11. MRS PONSONBY
12. FLORRIE WAINWRIGHT

The single series that spawned the greatest gallimaufry of crazy characters was undoubtedly *The Goon Show*. But who played who in that fast-paced flurry of fun?

13. THE FAMOUS ECCLES
14. BLUEBOTTLE
15. MAJOR GRYTPYPE-THYNNE
16. COUNT MORIARTY
17. LITTLE JIM
18. HENRY CRUN
19. MINNIE BANNISTER
20. THROAT
21. MAJOR DENIS BLOODNOCK
22. MATE

24: Title Fight

Get themselves a success on their hands and what do radio producers do? Change the title! And like as not that means the end of the success. Here are some famous radio series that suffered a title-change somewhere along the way. These are the original titles, you supply the later ones.

1. MONDAY NIGHT AT SEVEN
2. EDUCATING ARCHIE
3. IT'S THAT MAN AGAIN (ITMA)
4. CRAZY PEOPLE
5. MRS DALE'S DIARY
6. RAY'S A LAUGH
7. STUDIO STAND EASY
8. DANGER MEN AT WORK

The same kind of thing happens in the cinema. Films made in Hollywood often arrive in England with quite different titles from those they began with. Here are the British release titles of some well-remembered movies. Can you name the original titles?

9. ABBOTT AND COSTELLO MEET THE GHOSTS
10. STRANGE INCIDENT
11. THE MURDER IN THORNTON SQUARE
12. JOAN MEDFORD IS MISSING
13. MAN OF BRONZE
14. SECRET INTERLUDE
15. MARSHMALLOW MOON
16. TROUBLE CHASER
17. O'ROURKE OF THE ROYAL MOUNTED
18. THE STAR SAID NO

The same sort of thing happens in reverse, of course. British films get shown in America with strange new titles. Here are ten titles taken from American screens – can you put the original British titles to them?

19. A TALE OF FIVE WOMEN
20. ALL AT SEA
21. HOUSE OF FRIGHT
22. HORROR OF DRACULA
23. DIE, DIE, MY DARLING
24. MISTER V
25. MY SON THE VAMPIRE
26. FIVE MILLION YEARS TO EARTH
27. STAIRWAY TO HEAVEN
28. IVORY HUNTER

Here are ten more for the film fans. These are the titles of famous books and plays that were made into films. But, of course, the producers changed their titles before the films hit the cinemas. Can you name the names of the movie versions?

29. ALL IN GOOD TIME
30. BATS WITH BABY FACES
31. A SUITABLE CASE FOR TREATMENT
32. THAT UNCERTAIN FEELING
33. THE CLANSMAN
34. THE MALTESE FALCON
35. THE MOST DANGEROUS GAME
36. WEREWOLF OF PARIS
37. RING FOR CATTY
38. SANCTUARY

25: Big Sig

Clear your throats, folks, its time to air your tonsils as well as your knowledge. Every great radio show had its own original signature tune, and now's your chance to sing some. For every word you fill in correctly on the dotted lines, you win a point. So tap your tuning-forks and let's go.

1. IT'S MONDAY NIGHT AT SEVEN
   OH, CAN'T YOU ---- the ------
   THEY'RE TELLING YOU TO ---- AN ---- CHAIR
   AND SETTLE BY YOUR ---------
   LOOK AT YOUR ----- -----
   FOR MONDAY NIGHT AT SEVEN'S -- --- ---!

2. TAKE IT FROM HERE
   DON'T -- ---- WHEN YOU CAN
   TAKE IT FROM HERE
   WHY DON'T YOU ---- AND ----
   JOIN IN THE --- NOW
   THE SHOW HAS -----
   HALF AN HOUR OF --------- BECKONS
   EVERY ------ PACKED WITH -------!

3. WE'LL BE ---------- ------
   OH WHAT A --- FOR ------
   HE'S NO GOOD AT ---------
   HE HASN'T A ----
   HE THINKS THAT ------ ------
   STILL MAKE ------- ---
   WHAT A -------- ----- IS HE
   ---------- ------!

4. BAND WAGGON! COME ON AND ---- A ----
   UPON THE BAND WAGGON, IT'S A ---, BOYS!
   IT'S A GRAND WAGGON! COME ON AND ---- YOUR ----
   ABOARD THE BAND WAGGON -------- NOW, BOYS!

5. WHERE ---------- IS -----
   IT IS ----- TO BE ----
   IT'S ------ TO BE -------- LIKE ME!

6. ---- THAT ----! ---- THAT ----!
------ THAT ----! ------ THAT ---!
THE ---- ARE BACK IN THE ------
ROLL BACK THE ------ AND LET -------- GO!

7. COME TO THE ----------
COME TO THE ----
JUST TAKE A --- FROM --
THAT IS ----- TO --.

8. THE --- ---- ----
EXTENDING YOU A --------
AT THE --- ---- ----
WE HOLD OUR WEEKLY -------
IT'S SO ----- AND ---
THERE'S NOTHING TO ---
SO COME RIGHT IN AND LET US ----- YOUR --------
AWAY!

Have a rest now and see if you can remember the radio series whose signature tunes fitted around these phrases.

9. WHEN TROUBLE'S BREWING,
IT'S HIS DOING . . .

10. MUSIC, LAUGHTER, GAIETY, MELODY AND MIRTH,
SEE THE TATTOOED LADY AND YOU'LL GET YOUR
MONEY'S WORTH . . .

11. TIDDLE-IM-POM-POM . . .

12. HERE'S WISHING YOU ALL YOUR CARES
RIGHT UP ON THE SHELF . . .

13. AS YOU'RE SWINGING TO AND FRO,
IN YOUR HAMMOCK DOWN BELOW . . .

14. IT MAY BE POOR AND TUMBLE DOWN,
IT'S THE SUNDAY MORNING RENDEZVOUS OF LONDON TOWN . . .

15. DON'T GIVE IN! WEAR A GRIN!
DON'T LOOK LIKE A PASSPORT PHOTOGRAPH!

26: Pic Trick

Here's a list of pictures you've never seen in any movie reference book (not even the one I wrote: plug! plug!) – let alone in any cinema. Yet the titles look familiar. They are all genuine: it's just that they have got a little mixed. The first halves of the titles have got misplaced from the second halves. One point for every one you straighten out correctly. On the other hand, you may like these new titles so much you would sooner leave them the way they are now!

1. ABBOTT AND COSTELLO MEET PC 49
2. TICKET TO WONDERLAND
3. DOWN ROUND THE CORNER
4. IT ALWAYS RAINS ON MARGARET
5. ACTION OF THE LION
6. GEORGE AND SUNDAY
7. PAUL TEMPLE'S LODGER
8. APPOINTMENT WITH CAPTAIN KIDD
9. THE ADVENTURES OF EVELYN
10. THE BARRETTS OF OUTER SPACE
11. I'LL WALK WHERE I'M GOING
12. THE ANGEL WHO PAWNED HER TOMAHAWK
13. ANDROCLES AND THE TIGER
14. DANCE WITH ME HARP
15. ADAM AND VENUS
16. I KNOW WOMEN
17. HEAVEN IS HENRY
18. MY WIFE'S BESIDE YOU
19. PREHISTORIC TRIUMPH
20. ALICE IN WIMPOLE STREET
21. I MARRIED A MONSTER FROM MEMORY LANE

27: Tec Check

'Hats off to Edgar Wallace!' sang Stanley Lupino back in the twenties, and although nobody has yet sung a serenade to Sherlock Holmes or a cantata to Conan Doyle, everybody sings the praises of the great detectives of fiction. This detection section divides the chaps into chapters from catswhisker to cathode by way of the local library. First off, the wireless. Here are five famous radio detectors – can you remember who dun 'em?

1. PAUL TEMPLE
2. DICK BARTON
3. INSPECTOR HORNLEIGH
4. SHERLOCK HOLMES
5. P.C. 49

Yes, I know each part was probably played by at least ten different actors, but you just name the one who attained the most fame. This makes it easy on you, answer-wise (and on me, research-wise)! Now we'll try the same thing on film detectives.

6. PAUL TEMPLE
7. DICK BARTON
8. INSPECTOR HORNLEIGH
9. SHERLOCK HOLMES
10. P.C. 49

Moving right along but staying in the cinema, here are some famous American movie detectives. Again, just name the most famous actor in the role. To name them all would fill this quiz!

11. ELLERY QUEEN
12. CHARLIE CHAN
13. PHILO VANCE
14. PERRY MASON
15. BOSTON BLACKIE

Remember Simon Templar? He was better known as 'The Saint'. You've seen him in films and TV. Who played

16. THE SAINT IN AMERICAN FILMS
17. THE SAINT IN BRITISH FILMS
18. THE SAINT ON TV

So much for actors; now to authors. Who created the following famous fictional dicks?

19. LORD PETER WIMSEY
20. MISS MARPLE
21. MR MOTO
22. THE FALCON
23. JAMES BOND
24. PAUL TEMPLE
25. PERRY MASON
26. PHILO VANCE
27. THE SAINT
28. DICK BARTON

One famous fictional detective appeared in five different films, played by five different actors:

29. FAREWELL MY LOVELY
30. THE BIG SLEEP
31. THE LADY IN THE LAKE
32. THE HIGH WINDOW
33. MARLOWE

That last title was a dead giveaway! Now you have to add

34. THE NAME OF THE DETECTIVE
35. THE NAME OF THE AUTHOR

Too easy? So here comes the killer. Two of the films in the above list had different titles in America to those given, which were the British release titles. Name the original titles.

36. TITLE ONE
37. TITLE TWO

And just one more twist of the knife. Two of the stories had previously been filmed under different titles. What were they?

38. TITLE ONE
39. TITLE TWO

And still we haven't done with you. Scream while you torture your memory box to come up with the names of the detectives (we'll spare you the actors) who solved those two earlier mystery pictures.

40. DETECTIVE ONE
41. DETECTIVE TWO

Just like the cowboys, detectives have their 'comical side-kicks'. Ever since Sherlock Holmes had fun with Dr Watson no self-respecting sleuth would be caught in public without his stooge. Here are ten famous detectives' famous assistants; can you name their famous detectives?

42. THE RUNT
43. BIRMINGHAM
44. STEVE
45. ALGY LONGWORTH
46. DELLA STREET
47. INSPECTOR OSCAR PIPER
48. MR STRINGER
49. SNOWY
50. SERGEANT BINGHAM
51. JOLLY

Now one for the movie buffs. Who played each of those characters in the most popular movie versions? We'll run through them again so you have room to write them down.

52. THE RUNT
53. BIRMINGHAM
54. STEVE
55. ALGY LONGWORTH
56. DELLA STREET
57. INSPECTOR OSCAR PIPER
58. MR STRINGER
59. SNOWY
60. SERGEANT BINGHAM
61. JOLLY

Another famous film detective was the Thin Man, played by William Powell. He and his movie wife formed a perfect partnership that brought adult humour to the sex-starved thirties.

62. WHO PLAYED THE THIN MAN'S WIFE?

Oh, by the way, we forgot to tell you. Like all the great detective cases of novels, radio, and screen large or small, this episode contained a Deliberate Mistake. Did you spot it? There's a bonus Nostalgia Point at stake . . . and maybe five more!

28: Bill Thrill

In the good old golden days of the Music Hall no comic worth his sort of salt would be caught short without his Bill Matter. This was the line of type that was entered under every name on those great red-black-yellow posters outside the theatres. A catchy catch-phrase that summed up the star. You'd find them lined beneath the billing in the programme pages of *Radio Times*, too. Everybody had Bill Matter; it was written into the rules.

Here are a few famous fun phrases from those all-star days. One point for every name you can fit to the phrase.

1. THE CHEEKY CHAPPIE
2. ALMOST A GENTLEMAN
3. THE PRIME MINISTER OF MIRTH
4. THE LONG AND SHORT OF IT
5. THE PERFECT IDIOT
6. EVEN THEIR RELATIONS THINK THEY'RE FUNNY
7. A SONG, A SMILE, AND A PIANO
8. TWO MINDS WITHOUT A SINGLE THOUGHT
9. HE FILLS THE STAGE WITH FLAGS
10. THE VOICE OF INEXPERIENCE

And it wasn't only the comedians who had handy phrases; singers, too, boosted their box office with clever catchlines. One point for every singing star you can remember who billed themselves thus:

11. RADIO'S CAVALIER OF SONG
12. THE STREET SINGER
13. THE SMILING VOICE
14. THE VELVET FOG
15. THE TIGER RAGAMUFFINS
16. BRITAIN'S PREMIER LIGHT COMEDIAN
17. THE YODELING BRAKEMAN
18. THE CHOCOLATE COLOURED COON
19. THE WHITE-EYED KAFFIR
20. THE BRAZILIAN BOMBSHELL

29: Strip Trip (No. 2)

Here we go on our second trip to the strips. This time it isn't the kids comics – although us kids certainly read these cartoon capers in father's papers. Some of them were meant for our eyes, some of them weren't. Taking a curtain call are four queens of the strip, newspaper variety. Do you still keep a warm place in your heart for these girls of your youth?

1. Wide-eyed and winsome – so wide-eyed that she seldom showed a pupil – was this mump-cheeked waif. She brought her homespun philosophy to millions every day in the *Daily Mirror*. For one point, her name; for a second point, her *full* name – as it appeared in the pre-war papers.

2. This pretty little kid with the peek-a-boo bang brought the Lolita syndrome to the *Sunday Pictorial* years before the Nabakov novel. Point one: her name. Point two: the name of her strip before she took it over as star. Point three: her artist. Not so tough, because he was a famous pin-up king who also drew that newspaper's 'Dumb Blonde'.

3. The big panel first. The famous strip queen of the *Daily Mirror* – so easy we left her name in. You score points if you remember (a) her pet dog and (b) her boyfriend, the lucky lad she married.

4. The small picture is not Jane, although she looks like her. This girl appeared in the *Sunday Dispatch* after Jane was abandoned by her original artist. Points for (a) her name and (b) the name of the artist.

1

YEAH, I RECKON THERE'S NOTHIN' LIKE GOOD HONEST WORK TO MAKE YOU FERGET YA TROUBLES, MRS FRIZZLE...
ZIZZLE

2

3

JANE DISCARDS HER THIRD VEIL—
ONLY FOUR TO GO! OH GOSH! DO HURRY, CLANCY...

4

This page brings you another strip trip into the yellowed pages of yesterday's newspapers.

5. This half-pint hombre battled the baddies in the *Daily Mirror*. His allotted span was a full ten years, so you should certainly remember him. He had wild adventures with a mad inventor, if that's any help to you. It wasn't to him!

6. This barrel-bellied boor was the beetling, bottling butler in a strip in which the titular hero seldom, if ever, appeared! For your points, name the strip and the butler.

7. Stap me soothingly, serfs, if it isn't old – who? Yes, he was the scurvy squire who took over the strip we were talking about in question 6. Points as follows: the squire's name, the name of his country seat, and the name of his horrid harridan of a housekeeper whose jut-jawed jaw juts just to his right. The venue was the *Daily Mirror*.

8. Two panels from a famous office strip named – what? The headlined heroines are shown in panel two. Extra Nostalgia Point for the name of the boss (panel one). They functioned daily in *The Star*, and later in the *Evening News*. The artist was famous: can you remember his name? He also drew war maps.

CRIMINALS ARE GETTING TOO DERN RAMBUNCTIOUS...
...I OUGHTA CALL OUT TH' CAVALRY!
D.158.
???
GRR-GRR!
GRR-GRR!
LADY LAVINIA'S LOVER
ETHEL S.MELL
I'VE SENT JUNIOR OUT TO GET ME SOME BISCUITS.
THE BATTLE OF THE BULGE IS ON AGAIN.

5

6

7

8

Your third strip trip into the papers of the past features families, of sorts.

9. Here are three characters whose daily doings made readers of the *Daily Mirror* laugh for years. They were originally lodged on the sports page, as befits their surname. Name the strip, and the gent on the left, who was a permanent house guest. A third point for the name of the plump lump of cuddle he loved.

10. Another *Daily Mirror* family, of longer standing – although our panel catches them sitting down. They were collectively known as – what? Daughter Maisie is on the right. Second point for you if you remember the Christian name of the quizzical pater sat on the settee.

11. Below, doffing his topper, another family man. His monosyllabic cognomen was the title of his strip, and his take-over artist had an equally monosyllabic pseudonym. One point for each. His original artist was called J. Millar Watt. No points for that. Paper: the *Daily Sketch.*

12. Two panels from that ever-lasting *Daily Mirror* superhero, Garth. This musclebound gent spent his strip roaming the deeps of time and space, but wherever he landed he found the same two girls! Points for their names. The blonde one with the barefaced effrontery is shown here; the other lass was usually more modest, yet darker of hair and intent.

WILL YOU—
EXCUSE HIM JUST A JIFF WHILE I HAVE A WORD WITH HIM
WELL REALLY, MR. F!

9

...and then she said—"How's Maisie?" and I said "didn't you know?—She's got TWINS!"...
SH!—JULIAN HATES PEOPLE TALKING WHILE THE NEWS IS ON!

10

WE SHOULD ESCAPE—AND SMOKE OUT THIS NEST OF VIPERS!

I'LL WAIT!

11

BUT HOW, GARTH?—WE HAVE NO SHIP—AND THE ISLE IS IN THE HANDS OF THE SPANIARDS!

12

Winding up our strip trip we take a deep dive down memory lane to look at some of the strip characters us kids were supposed to read – the heroes of the newspapers' kiddies' corners.

13. This chubby little bear pranked in the pages of the *Daily Mirror*, post-war. He was – and is – a television hero. His name, and the name of his master, will win you two easy points.

14. A mouse and a duck: simple stuff, but of such was the first British newspaper strip for children wrought. They were revived after the war, from which period our portrait is taken. Name the mouse (clue: he has a knot in his tail), name the duck, and name the patient lady who looked after them. Also, name their newspaper.

15. Here's a rare sight, a panel from a pre-war Sunday paper strip featuring a family of coloured folks. The strip was named after the male and female of the clan, and a second point is for the name of the paper. The name of the artist was Wilfred Haughton.

16. Back to the *Daily Mirror* for the best remembered paper pets of them all. Name them (one point), and name the famous children's club which was run by the rabbit! (another point). The artist signed every strip, so you should remember his name, too (third point).

13

14

15

LET'S PLAY GOLF
WHAT AM YOU GOING TO DO WID DE SAND ?
SAND
HE SAID WE AM GOING TO MAKE DE 'TEE' WID IT !

16

SHE'S IN THE BASKET
I HOPE SO!

30: Number Lumber Number Two

Our next little number is another number lumber. This time it's the movie buffs' turn, for these aren't musical numbers we are reminding you of. They are genuine number-type numbers, in genuine movie-type movie titles. Trouble is, the movies all have the wrong numbers! Your job, for one point a time, is to sort them out into their right numbers. On the other hand, you may prefer to leave them as they are: they sound more interesting this way!

1. $23\frac{1}{2}$ OF OUR AIRCRAFT IS MISSING
2. 2000 KEYS TO BALDPATE
3. 60 O'CLOCK HIGH
4. 2 GLORIOUS YEARS
5. 1 FATHOMS DEEP
6. 13 CABALLEROS
7. 40 FACES WEST
8. 6 GRAVES TO CAIRO
9. 20 SHOOTIN' SHERIFF
10. 100 MULE TEAM
11. 50 YEARS BEFORE THE MAST
12. 40,000 MEN AND A GIRL
13. 12 RUE MADELEINE
14. 10 LITTLE MOTHERS
15. 3 WOMEN
16. 4 HORSEMEN
17. 9 GENTLEMEN FROM WEST POINT
18. 7 LIVES ARE NOT ENOUGH
19. 5 HOURS LEAVE
20. 16 ROADS TO TOWN

There are a number of acts that go by numbers, too. Can you name the following? Number one point for each name.

21. THE TWO LESLIES
22. THE THREE STOOGES
    Extra Nostalgia Points if you know their real names.
23. THE FOUR MARX BROTHERS
    Again, extra Nostalgia Points if you know their real names.
24. THE FIVE LITTLE PEPPERS
25. THE SIX HITS AND A MISS
    (No, no – not their names – just who or what they were.)
26. THE SEVEN DWARFS

31: Series Queries

Back in the Odeon days of old there was one kind of film that brought us back again and again. This was the series film, usually belonging to the class of 'B' production, which had a regular repertory cast of character actors. They don't make movies like these any more: they make TV series like them instead.

1. *Blondie*, the daily strip cartoon by Chic Young, was a perfectly cast series. Who played the bubble-headed housewife lead? (1) Who played Dagwood, her husband? (1) And what was their incredible surname? (1) Can you remember the names of their children? There was a boy, whose original name was 'Baby Dumpling'. He grew up into . . . (1). His little sister had a cute name, too . . . (1) Finally, there was the family dog. Her name was . . . ? (1)

2. MGM had a marvellous family saga going for them in the what family? (1) Dad was a judge, and was played by whom? (1) Extra Nostalgia Point for the name of the actor who played the judge in the very first film in the series. (1) The star of the series was young . . . (1) who played the son, named . . . (1). His girl friend was called . . . (1) and she was played by . . . (1). Mum, or as he would call her, mom, was played by . . . (1).

3. This gang of juvenile delinquents was known variously as the . . . Kids (1) and, the . . . Boys (1). Originally they were called the . . . Kids (1), after their appearance in that famous play and film. A minor studio called . . . (1) made the series, and starred . . . (1) as the ageing leader of the gang. His equally ancient junior was . . . (1), and the characters they played in the pictures were . . . (1) and . . . (1). (Extra Nostalgia Points if you can give their full names, and one more for the milk bar where they used to hang out.)

4. Back to the big studios for this series. MGM made a long saga out of the affairs of Blair Hospital, originally written about in novels by . . . (1). Titular star was Dr . . . (1) played by . . . (1), but the scene was stolen by Dr . . . (1), played from his wheelchair by crusty . . . (1). The nurse in the case, Mary Lamont, was played by pretty . . . (1). After the original star left the series, several new stars were called in to assist the old doc. One point for each you can name, and another for naming the one that eventually 'stuck'.

5. The Sherlock Holmes series was produced by a studio usually associated with horror films. Name it (1), and name the two stars who played Holmes and Watson (2). Holmes' arch-enemy Professor . . . (1) appeared four times in the series, and each time he was played by a different actor. Can you name them all? (4) Two more regulars in the series were . . . (1) as cocky cockney Inspector . . . (1), and . . . (1) as Holmes' dumpy housekeeper, Mrs . . . (1).

32: Paper Caper

Open up an old, old newspaper and what do you find? Old, old chips. But smiling through the vinegar stains come the names that once were as familiar as Katherine Whitehorn and Angus McGill, and you know how familiar they are! (Actually they are just good friends!) Here are a handful of newspaper names and magazine writers from the yellowed press of yore. Unscramble each for one point.

1. EVELYN VEAL
2. COLLIE HICKEY
3. BIP WIGNALL
4. REG PARES
5. NAT BARRINGTON
6. IRENE KNOX
7. C. A. WHITELEY
8. JONAH LEJEUNE
9. WILLIAM HOME
10. TREVOR GUBBINS

33: Sport Short

Leslie Welch the Memory Man is the chap to go to for your sporting nostalgia, not me. However, one or two, in fact a round ten, names with sporting connections do lurk about in my nostalgic subconscious. Thus, even if you are as non-sporting a type as I, you should still score a full ten points on sorting out these notable names.

1. TOMMY BRADMAN
2. PRIMO ROCKNE
3. MAX CAMPBELL
4. STEVE SCHMELLING
5. KNUTE CARNERA
6. BLUEY LOUIS
7. MALCOLM FARR
8. DON DONOGHUE
9. JACK WILKINSON
10. JOE JOHNSON

34: Ad Mad

Advertisements have always played an important part in our lives, even before – especially before – ITV. The old ad campaigns used to be much more fun than they are today, now that advertising is a so-called science. Remember Gillroy's super colour cartoon posters for . . . ah, but let that be the first question in our checklist of poster posers. One point for every product you can put into place.

1. MY GOODNESS MY ...
2. WALK THE ... WAY
3. GIVE HER A RING. MAKE IT A ...
4. THAT ... FEELING
5. ... PREVENTS THAT SINKING FEELING
6. THAT'S ... THAT WAS!
7. AH! ... !
8. TEN MINUTES TO WAIT SO MINE'S A ...
9. ... PUTS A SPRING IN YOUR STEP
10. WHERE'S GEORGE? GONE TO ...

Other catchphrases did not include the names of the products they were plugging. Can you remember what went with:

11. LET ME BE YOUR FATHER
12. FOUR FOR YOUR FRIENDS
13. WHEN IT'S NO SMOKING BY ORDER
14. THE GRASSHOPPER MIND
15. NOT TOO LITTLE, NOT TOO MUCH, BUT JUST RIGHT
16. THERE ARE DIFFERENT LEVELS OF SLEEP JUST AS THERE ARE DIFFERENT LEVELS OF CONSCIOUSNESS
17. IVORY CASTLES
18. GRETA COLDAY (or ROLAND BUTTER)
19. BREAD AND MILK AT A PARTY? HOW UNJUST! HOW AWFUL!
20. THEY COME AS A BOON AND A BLESSING TO MEN

Long before the first television commercial jingled its tingling fresh taste on British TV, back in those far away days of 1939, we listened regularly to similar songs that sang the praises of products which ranged from Rinso to Palmolive by way of Bi-So-Dol. These were broadcast to Britain somewhat illegally by Radio Luxembourg and her sister stations, Radios Normandy, Poste-Parisien, and even Athlone.

Here are a few phrases from those jaunty, jolly jingles, which I remember. Do you remember what they were advertising?

21. HIGH O'ER THE FENCE,
O'ER THE FENCE LEAPS SUNNY JIM,
. . . IS THE FOOD,
IS THE FOOD THAT RAISES HIM!

22. GET OUT OF BED,
BE HAPPY AND SO,
MAKE YOURSELF A NICE PERSON TO KNOW!

23. AT GAMES AND SPORTS WE'RE MORE THAN KEEN,
NO MERRIER CHILDREN TO BE SEEN,
BECAUSE WE ALL DRINK . . .
WE'RE HAPPY GIRLS AND BOYS!

24. HURRAH FOR . . .
WHAT A DELIGHTFUL SMELL!
IT'S THE STUFF THAT EVERY SELF-RESPECTING
GROCER OUGHT TO SELL!

35: Flicks Mix

Here comes another name game and we are up to our mixed-up tricks again. This time it is film stars who suffer. Well, they were stars to those who liked 'B' pictures as much as, if not more than, the 'A' pictures they were meant to support.

First, sort out these ladies into their correct names.

1. LYNN LANE
2. NAN ANKERS
3. WENDY BARI
4. JEAN SAVAGE
5. PRISCILLA PARKER
6. JULIE BARRIE
7. ELLEN GREY
8. EVELYN BISHOP
9. RUTH DREW
10. ANN HUSSEY

And for our second feature, sort out these second feature gentlemen.

11. LEON COLONNA
12. PEDRO DE STROHEIM
13. JERRY ERROL
14. TOM TOOMBES
15. CHESTER COWAN
16. ERICH VON CLUTE
17. ANDREW CORDOBA
18. EDWARD LITEL
19. JOHN NORRIS
20. JEROME NEAL

36: Strip Trip (No. 3)

No pictures for this strip trip: only mental ones, which I'm sure will be conjured up in your recall department as you read off these nostalgic names – Keyhole Kate, Big Eggo, Korky the Cat, Desperate Dan! That was just to warm you up, get you into the right mood for another in-depth dip into the wonderful world of children's comics.

The cartoon characters in our old comics always had catchy names, and even catchier subtitles. Can you remember the nutty names that went with these daft descriptions?

1. THE CLOCKWORK BOY
2. THE WONKY WAITER
3. THE COMICAL COOK
4. THE ROLLICKING ROMANS
5. THE FEARLESS FLY
6. HE'S 700 YEARS OLD

This next bunch should be even easier to remember: their captions actually rhymed with their names.

7. THE STRONG MAN'S DAUGHTER
8. YOUR BARBER PAL
9. THE CUTE HINDOO
10. THE SNEEZING CAESAR
11. AND HIS COCKATOO
12. AND HER GREAT BIG POODLE
13. HE'S A BIG-A-DA-FLOP
14. HE'S SMART AND SLICK
15. HE'S A PROPER SCREAM

Other characters had complete couplets after their names. Who fitted the following?

16. HIS WHISKERS NEAT REACH TO HIS FEET
17. FUN JUST LINGERS ROUND HIS FINGERS
18. ONE TON OF FUN
19. THE STRONG-ARM SCHOOL-MARM
20. HE BEATS THE BAND AND SHAKES THE WHOLE OF REDSKIN LAND

Magic always played a great part in those magical old comic papers. Who had:

21. A MAGIC CIGAR
22. A MAGIC PATCH
23. A MAGIC BROLLY
24. A MAGIC BOOK
25. MAGIC LOLLIPOPS

Actually, to be fair, the little lad who had a jar full of those last-named lollies never had a name. But he did have a catchline. What was it?

Gangs are great stuff for comics. 'Lord Snooty and his Pals' have been in *The Beano* right since the very first issue. So you ought to be able to name the gang, didn't you? Ah-ah! Don't go looking them up in your kid's current copy: the constitution has changed since our day.

26. NAME LORD SNOOTY'S PALS
27. WHAT IS LORD SNOOTY'S REAL NAME?

'Lord Snooty and his Pals' operate on the 'Our Gang' principal. In fact, that famous film team used to function in a companion comic, *The Dandy*. Can you name the component parts of 'Our Gang' as it appeared in that comic?

28. NAME OUR GANG
29. NAME OUR GANG'S FILM PRODUCER

The cartoonist who originally drew both Lord Snooty and Our Gang was one of the few who was ever allowed to sign his strips, an event so rare in British comics you should easily recall his name.

30. WHO DREW LORD SNOOTY AND OUR GANG?

Another famous gang, although Mrs Bruin would have held her hands – sorry, paws – high in horror at the use of the word, was 'The Bruin Boys'. This well-dressed menagerie occupied the front page of *The Rainbow* and its colourful companion, *Tiger Tim's Weekly*, for more years than we know. Can you reel off the names of the Bruin Boys? You've already got one of them . . .

31. NAME THE BRUIN BOYS

It would be too much to ask of your NQ to name their feminine counterparts, animal by animal that is, but do you remember what they were called? Tiger Tilly was their leader.

32. NAME THE OPPOSITE OF THE BRUIN BOYS
33. WHICH COMIC WERE THEY FEATURED IN?

37: Hero Zero

Do you remember the thrill of passing your tuppence over the newsagent's counter and taking up in return a thick, 28-page package of print entitled *The Champion?* Or *The Wizard?* Or possibly *The Triumph?* One short-lived one was *The Buzzer*, a great bargain: 32 pages for 2d! These were the boys' papers, tuppenny bloods we called them. Seven Star Stories, strips in the middle, and Order Next Week's Issue Now, Chums and Be Sure of getting your Grand Free Gift!

Here are more than Seven Star Story heroes, only our silly printer has gone and mixed them up again, lads! Still, you'll soon sort 'em out, won't you? Especially as there's one point, Grand and Free, for every name you get right!

1. THE WOLF OF WOLFF
2. BIG BAD BLAKE
3. SOLO STIFF
4. CAPTAIN OF KABUL
5. STRANG SAPPER
6. SEXTON HAWKE
7. THE BIG DANE
8. BLACK JUSTICE
9. THE LAUGHING PHANTOM
10. DIXON FLYNN
11. THE BLACKFRIARS BUCCANEER
12. COLWYN CAREW
13. MAD THE TERRIBLE
14. ROCKFIST SOLOMON
15. FIREWORKS ROGAN

38: Phrase Craze

Before we bid a final farewell to the comic paper scene, here's a quick quiz that links strips to stars. Remember *Film Fun?* That comic used to feature film stars as strip cartoon characters. But, being a comic, Eddie the Happy Editor always put a typical strip caption under each star's names. Can you recall the movie comedians who were billed as:

1. THE MOST POPULAR PAIR ON THE PICTURES
2. THE WHIMSICAL WAG
3. MEET THE MERRIEST OF MOVIELAND'S MIRTHMAKERS
4. THE FAMOUS FELLOW OF THE FILMS
5. THE FILM FAN'S FAVOURITE FUN-MAKER
6. THE FAMOUS RADIO PICTURE STARS
7. THE SCREAM OF THE SCREEN
8. THE FAMOUS LAUGHTER-MAKER OF THE SCREEN
9. STARS OF UNIVERSAL PICTURES

39: Finale Parlay

Well, folks, the clock on the wall says 'Gifford, that's all!', to paraphrase a phrase popularised by – who? No, I'll give you that one: Ralph 'Muff-it' Moffatt. (Who?) One Nostalgia Point to me!

Here, before we part company, is one last little list, a collection of classic farewells, goodbyes, signoffs and suchlike. One point for each one you can put a name to.

1. GOODNIGHT CHILDREN . . . EVERYWHERE!
2. GOODNIGHT EVERYBODY, AND CAN YOU HEAR ME, MOOTHER?
3. GOODNIGHT, GOOD NEET, AND CHEERIO . . .
4. WELL GOO'NIGHT EV'RY-BAHDY.
5. ON BE'ALF OF ME AN' THE BOYS I'D LIKE TO SAY 'THANKS FER LIST'NIN'!
6. GOOD NIGHT, AND THANKS FOR THE USE OF YOUR LOUDSPEAKERS!
7. GOODNIGHT EVERYONE, AND HERE'S TO THE NEXT TIME!
8. SO-LONG, CHUMS – LUMMY I DON'T ARF BUMP INTO SOME FUNNY OLD HOWDYEDO'S, DON'T I?
9. SO-LONG, THEEER!
10. (sing this one)
    GOODNIGHT, GOODNIGHT, GOODNIGHT, GOODNIGHT, GOODNI-I-IGHT,
    GOODNIGHT, GOODNIGHT, GOODNIGHT, GOODNIGHT, GOODNIGHT!
    (repeat and fade slowly into the distance).

ANSWERS

Total possible points given at the end of each game.

1: Start Part

1. Jimmy Edwards (1)
2. Bernard Miles (1)
3. Wilfred Pickles (1)
4. Jack Warner (1)
5. Syd Walker (1)
6. Pa Glum (Jimmy Edwards) (1)
7. Gillie Potter (1)
8. Robert Moreton (1)
9. Leon Cortez (1)
10. Big Bill Campbell (1)
11. Gracie Fields (1)
12. Max Miller (1)
13. Elsie and Doris Waters (1)
14. Leslie Sarony (1)
    also The Two Leslies (1)
15. Jimmy O'Dea (1)
16. Carroll Levis (1)
17. Ronald Frankau (1)
18. Anne Zeigler and Webster Booth (1)
19. Jack Benny (1)
20. Albert Whelan (1)
    He claimed it was the first ever signature tune. (1)
21. Say It With Music (1)
22. Whispering (1)
23. Somebody Stole My Girl (1)
24. On The Air (1)
25. Henry Hall had not one, but two: he opened with It's Just The Time For Dancing (1) and closed with Here's To The Next Time (1)
26. Cherokee (1)
27. I'm Gettin' Sentimental Over You (1)
28. Nightmare (1)
29. Auld Lang Syne (1)
30. Moonlight Serenade (1)

31. 'We know we're modest when we say (1)
That when we play (1)
That we're gonna getcha (1)
In such a way (1)
That it can't upsetcha! Betcha! (1)

Total: 38

2: Dance Chance

1. Troise (1)
2. Macari (1)
3. Billy Merrin (1)
4. Henry Hall (1)
5. Sid Roy (1)
6. Geraldo (1)
7. Big Bill Campbell (1)
8. Bertini (1)
9. Sydney Kyte (1)
10. Carroll Gibbons (1)
11. Ivy Benson (1)
12. Anona Winn (1)
13. Josephine Bradley (1)
14. Red McKenzie (1)
15. Red Nicholls (1)
16. Rudy Vallee (1)
17. Ray Ventura (1)
18. Carson Robison (1)
19. Andy Iona (1)
20. Andy Kirk (1)
21. City Slickers (1)
22. Nitwits (1)
23. Hayseeds (1)
24. Crackpots (1)
25. Natural Seven (1)
26. Mad Hatters (1)
27. Kosher Jammers (1)
28. Garbage Men (1)
29. Harry Parry and his Radio Rhythm Club Sextet (1)
30. Johnny Claes and his Claepigeons (1)
31. Johnny Denis and his Ranchers (1)

32. Sid Lipton and his Grosvenor House Band (1)
33. Leon Cortez and his Coster Pals (1)
34. Frank Biffo and his Brass Quintet (1)
35. Nat Gonella and his Georgians (1)
36. J. H. Squire and his Celeste Octet (1)
37. Ciro Rimal and his Rumbaland Muchachos (1) (Yes, that one was right all the time!)

Total: 37

3: Name Game

1. Barbara Stanwyck (1)
2. Joan Crawford (1)
3. Loretta Young (1)
4. Mary Astor (1)
5. Veronica Lake (1)
6. Fredric March (1)
7. Cary Grant (1)
8. Stan Laurel (1)
9. Danny Kaye (1)
10. Ray Milland (1)
11. Fred Astaire (1)
    Ginger Rogers (1)
12. Mickey Rooney (1)
    Judy Garland (1)
13. Boris Karloff (1)
    Bela Lugosi (1)
14. Phyllis Calvert (1)
    Stewart Granger (1)
15. Roy Rogers (1)
    Dale Evans (1)
16. Anne Heywood (1)
17. Greta Gynt (1)
18. Margaret Lockwood (1)
19. Kay Kendall (1)
20. Michael Caine (1)
21. Muriel Pavlow (1)
    Derek Farr (1)
22. Dulcie Gray (1)
    Michael Denison (1)

23. Helen Cherry (1)
    Trevor Howard (1)
24. Kay Hammond (1)
    John Clements (1)
25. Lilli Palmer (1)
    Rex Harrison (1)
26. Margaret Johnston (1)
    Laurence Harvey (1)
27. Viriginia McKenna (1)
    Bill Travers (1)
28. Jean Simmons (1)
    Stewart Granger (1)
29. Joan Collins (1)
    Anthony Newley (1)
30. Patricia Medina (1)
    Richard Greene (1)
31. Richard Arlen (1)
32. Robert Lowery (1)
33. Warren William (1)
34. Jane Frazee (1)
35. Helen Twelvetrees (1)
36. Douglas Fairbanks (1)
37. John Barrymore (1)
38. Mary Pickford (1)
39. Richard Dix (1)
40. Pola Negri (1)
41. Gracie Fields (1)
42. George Robey (1)
43. Fanny Brice (1)
44. Harry Tate (1)
45. Max Miller (1)
46. Frank Randle (1)
47. Carl Brisson (1)
48. Lupino Lane (1)
49. Al Jolson (1)
50. Sandy Powell (1)
51. Name of a comedian (1)
    and a jazz musician (1)
52. Name of a comedian (1)
    and a golf champion (1)
53. Name of a British film star (1)
    and an American film actor (1)

54. Name of a British band leader (1)
 and an American film actor (1)
55. Name of a composer (1)
 and a pop singer (1)
56. Name of a British dance band leader (1)
 and an American film actor (1)
57. Name of a hillbilly singer (1)
 and a pop singer (1)
58. They were all followed into show business by their 'juniors'. (1)

Total: 79

4: Initial Entry

1. J. (1)
2. C. (1)
3. J. (1)
4. S. (1)
5. P. (1)
6. E. (1)
7. E. (1)
8. B. (1)
9. S. (1)
10. Q. (1)
11. B. (1)
12. E. (1)
13. E.E. (2)
14. K.T. (2)
15. B.S. (2)
16. J.G. (2)
17. O.Z. (2)
18. P.J. (2)
19. F.H. (2)
20. C.H. (2)
21. A.B. (2)
22. E.V.H. (3)
23. W. (1)

Total: 23

5: Mister Twister

1. Robb Wilton (1)
   Mr Muddlecombe JP (1)
2. Laidman Browne (1)
   Ray's A Laugh (1)
3. Ralph De Rohan (1)
   Toytown (1)
4. Hugh Morton (1)
   Life With The Lyons (1)
5. Horace Percival (1)
   Life With The Lyons (1)
6. Richard Hearne (1)
   Caught you: he was never a radio series. (1)
7. Dorothy Summers (1)
   It's That Man Again (1)
8. Mabel Constanduros (1)
   The Buggins Family (1)
9. Nobody: she never actually spoke. (1)
   Band Waggon (1)
10. Maurice Denham (1)
    It's That Man Again (1)
11. Bob Pearson (1)
    Ray's A Laugh (1)
12. Rex Jamison (1)
    London Lights (1)

Total: 24

6: Bracket Racket

1. Gabby (1)
2. Fuzzy (1)
3. Harry (1)
4. Big Boy (1)
5. Bill (1)
6. Jack (1)
7. Crazylegs (1)
8. Hubert (1)
9. Mr Piano (1)

10. Umbrage (1)
11. Jizz (1)
12. Stinker (1)
13. Uke (1)
14. Fingers (1)

Total: 14

7: Middle Riddle

1. Marion (1)
2. Stamp (1)
3. Seth (1)
4. Howard (1)
5. Mae (1)
6. Havelock (1)
7. Hall (1)
8. Hyde (1)
9. Desmond (1)
10. Murray (1)

Total: 10

8: None Fun

1. Frank Sinatra (1)
2. Lauren Bacall (1)
3. Lizbeth Scott (1)
4. Vicki Dougan (1)
5. Marie McDonald (1)

Total: 5

9: Same Name

1. Freddie Mills (1)
   The Mills Brothers (1)

2. Big Bill Campbell (1)
   Campbell's Soup (1)
3. The Carter Family (1)
   Carter's Little Liver Pills (1)
4. Bob Monkhouse (1)
   A Monk House (1)
5. The Lyons Family (1)
   Lyons Corner House (1)
6. An Andrews Sister (1)
   Andrews Liver Salt (1)
7. Olivia De Havilland (1)
   De Havilland (1)
8. Edward G. Robinson (1)
   Robinson's Barley Water (1)
9. W. C. Fields (1)
   W. C. (1)
10. Fredric March (1)
    March Composer (1)

Total: 20

10: Nick Trick

1. Oliver (1)
2. Ellington (1)
3. Basie (1)
4. Hines (1)
5. Beginner (1)
6. Billy Holiday (1)
7. Paul Whiteman (1)
8. Earl Hines (1)
9. Stitt (1)
10. Ory (1)
11. Dodds (1)
12. Stan Kenton (1)
13. Louis Armstrong (1)
14. Morton (1)
15. Huddie Leadbetter (1)
16. Herman (1)
17. Manone (1)

18. Spanier (1)
19. Bregman (1)
20. Hucko (1)
21. Johnson (1)
22. Page (1)
23. Elman (1)
24. Singleton (1)
25. Waller (1)
26. Gaillard (1)
27. Hayes (1)
28. Ennis (1)
29. Rogers (1)

Total: 29

11: Wrong Song

1. Fred Astaire	Top Hat (1)
2. Teresa Brewer	Music, Music, Music (1)
3. Bing Crosby	Pennies from Heaven (1)
4. Doris Day	It's Magic (1)
5. Billy Eckstine	My Foolish Heart (1)
6. Eddie Fisher	Any Time (1)
7. Judy Garland	Over the Rainbow (1)
8. Phil Harris	That's What I Like About the South (1)
9. Burl Ives	The Riddle Song (1)
10. Allan Jones	The Donkey Serenade (1)
11. Kay Kyser	Horses Don't Bet On People (1)
12. Frankie Laine	Mule Train (1)
13. Ella Mae Morse	Cow Cow Boogie (1)
14. Gertrude Neisen	I Wanna Get Married (1)
15. Helen O'Connell	Six Lessons From Madame La Zonga (1)
16. Pattie Page	How Much Is That Dog In The Window (1)
17. Johnnie Ray	The Little White Cloud That Cried (1)
18. Dinah Shore	Tess's Torch Song (1)
19. Martha Tilton	G'Bye Now (1)

20. Rudy Vallee	The Whiffenpoof Song (1)
21. Fats Waller	My Very Good Friend the Milkman (1)
22. Les Allen	Little Man You've Had a Busy Day (1)
23. Al Bowlly	Auf Wiedersehen My Dear (1)
24. Dorothy Carless	Room 504 (1)
25. Beryl Davis	My Heart Goes Crazy (1)
26. Ray Ellington	The Three Bears (1)
27. Gracie Fields	Little Old Lady (1)
28. Carroll Gibbons	Comes Love (1)
29. Leslie Hutchinson	These Foolish Things (1)
30. Dick James	Robin Hood (1)
31. Kathie Kaye	Jimmy Unknown (1)
32. Vera Lynn	We'll Meet Again (1)
33. Scotty McHarg	To Each His Own (1)
34. Jessie Matthews	Over My Shoulder (1)
35. Monty Norman	Answer Me (1)
36. Donald Peers	In a Shady Nook (1)
37. Monte Rey	So Deep Is The Night (1)
38. Dorothy Squires	The Gipsy (1)
39. Bruce Trent	The Bells of Saint Mary's (1)
40. Bertha Willmott	Beer Barrel Polka (1)
41. Yana	Climb Up The Wall (1)

Total: 41

12: Number Lumber

1. Five (1)
2. One Dozen (1)
3. One (1)
4. Three (1)
5. Twenty-one (1)
6. Eleven; (1)
   Ten (1)
7. Seven (1)
8. Six (1)
9. Ten (1)
10. Forty Fousand (1)

11. In Cherry Blossom Lane (1)
12. I love you I do (1)
13. 'Cos jam don't shake like that! (1)
14. Barnacle Bill the Sailor (1)
15. Sioux City Sue (1)
16. Laura (1)
17. Nancy with the laughing face. (1)
18. You don't know and I don't know
    And neither does the cow! (1)
19. Tennessee is not very far. (1)
20. So my poor old pop will know it's time for him to stop. (1)
21. Black (1)
22. Pink (1)
23. Green (1)
24. Yellow (1)
25. Purple (1)
26. White (1)
27. Scarlet (1)
28. Orange (1)
29. Red (1)
30. Blue (1)

Total: 31

13: Absurd Word

1. Chick-a-la-romey in a banonika (1)
2. And little lambsey tivey (1)
3. Foo-de-racky-sacky (1)
4. Dottem wottem choo! (1)
5. Putti-putti (1)

Total: 5

14: Keyboard Chord

1. Charlie Kunz (1)
2. Carroll Gibbons (1)
3. Kay Cavendish (1)

4. Arthur Young (1)
5. Patricia Rossborough (1)
6. Ronald Gourlay (1)
7. Billy Mayerl (1)
8. Jan August (1)
9. Carmen Cavallaro (1)
10. Tony Lowry (1)
11. Rawicz and Landauer (1)
12. Reub Silver and Marion Day (1)
13. Harry S. Pepper and Doris Arnold (1)
14. Jose and Amparo Iturbi (1)
15. Ivor Moreton and Dave Kaye (1)
16. Terence Casey (1)
17. Reginald Dixon (1)
18. Sandy MacPherson (1)
19. Robinson Cleaver (1)
20. Robin Richmond (1)
21. Bobby Pagan (1)
22. Florence De Jong (1)
23. Sidney Torch (1)
24. Quentin MacLean (1)
25. Reginald Foort (1)
26. Billy Bennett: all the rest play the piano (1)

Total: 26

15: Double Trouble

1. Mooney (1)
2. Williams (1)
3. Wilson (1)
   (No marks if you put Woolsey! They were American film stars.)
4. Dwyer (1)
5. Dean (1)
   Breen (1)
6. Bud (1)
   Chesney (1)
7. Jimmy (1)
   Teddy (1)

8. Charlie (1)
   Jimmy (1)
9. Teamed together they formed 'The Crazy Gang' (1)
10. Claude Dampier (1)
11. Claude Hulbert (1)
12. Billy Caryll (1)
13. Nat Mills (1)
14. Rupert Hazell (1)
15. They were married to each other: all husband-and-wife acts. (1)
16. Tommy Handley (1)
    Ronald Frankau (1)
17. Billy Bennett (1)
    Albert Whelan (1)
    originally James Carew (1)
18. B. C. Hilliam (1)
    Malcolm MacEachern (1)
19. Alex McGill (1)
    Fred Yule (1)
20. Ronald Frankau (1)
    Tommy Handley (1)

Total: 30

16: Three Spree

1. Farrell (1)
2. Nevard (1)
3. Me! (1)

Total: 3

17: Fame Game

1. Pattie Andrews (1)
2. Bill Kenny (1)
3. Bing Crosby (1)

4. Connee Boswell (1)
5. Ted Healy (who left The Three Stooges to go solo) (1)

Total: 5

18: Team Scream

1. Laurel and Hardy (1)
2. Crosby and Hope (1)
3. Monkhouse and Goodwin (1)
4. Muir and Norden (1)
5. Wheeler and Woolsey (1)
6. Abbott and Costello (1)
7. The Western Brothers (1)
8. Martin and Lewis (1)
9. Mooney and King (1)
10. Waters (1)
11. Frank and Ernest (1)
12. Amos and Andy (1)
13. Lucan and MacShane (1)
14. Revnell and West (1)
15. Morecambe and Wise (1)
16. Haver and Lee (1)
17. Stanelli and Edgar (1)
18. Noni and Partner (1)
19. Bennett and Williams (1)
20. Bergen and McCarthy (1)
21. Scott and Whaley (1)
22. Haver and Lee (1)
23. Charlie Drake and Jack Edwards (1)
24. Elsie and Doris Waters (1)

Total: 24

19: West Test

1. Trigger (1)
2. Champion (1)

3. Tarzan (1)
4. White Flash (1)
5. Tony (1)
6. Black Jack (1)
7. George 'Gabby' Hayes (1) or Andy Clyde (1)
8. George 'Gabby' Hayes (1)
9. Smiley Burnette (1)
10. Snub Pollard (1)
11. Raymond Hatton (1)
12. Leo Carrillo (1)
13. Richard Martin (1)
14. Al 'Fuzzy' St John (1)
15. Max 'Alibi' Terhune (1)
16. Silver (1)
17. Tonto (1)
18. Roy Barcroft (1)
19. I. Stanford Jolley (1)
20. Tom London (1)
21. Kenne Duncan (1)
22. George Chesebro (1)
23. Morris Ankrum (1)
24. Charles King (1)
25. Tristram Coffin (1)
26. Bells of San Angelo (1)
27. Yodelin' Kid from Pine Ridge (1)
28. Home in Wyomin' (1)
29. Man from Music Mountain (1)
30. Springtime in the Rockies (1)
31. Heart of the Golden West (1)
32. In Old Caliente (1)
33. Pals of the Golden West (1)
34. Down Mexico Way (1)
35. Blue Montana Skies (1)
36. Wilson (1)
37. Knight (1)
38. Hayes (1)
39. Jones (1)
40. Gibson (1)
41. Elliott (1)
42. Barry (1)
43. Lane (1)
44. Crabbe (1)

45. Carson (1)
46. Roy Rogers (1)
47. Trigger (1)
48. Dick Foran (1)
49. Champion (1)
50. Rex Allen (1)
51. Buster Crabbe (1)
52. Dale Evans (1)
53. Lulubelle and Scotty (1)
54. Bob Nolan and the Sons of the Pioneers (1)
55. The Hoosier Hotshots (1)
56. The Weaver Brothers and Elviry (1)
57. Foy Willing and the Riders of the Purple Sage (1)

Total: 58

20: Strip Trip (No. 1)

1. Weary Willie and Tired Tim (1)
   Chips (1)
   Illustrated Chips (1)
2. Basil and Bert (1)
   Jester (1)
   Blue (later pink) (1)
3. Laurie and Trailer (2)
   Prince Oddsocksz (1)
   Serge Pantz (1)
   Chips (1)
4. Constable Cuddlecook (1)
   Jester (1)
   Inspector Flipflap (1)
5. Peggy the Pride of the Force (1)
   Larks (1)
6. Ben and Bert (1)
   Funny Wonder (1)
7. Pitch and Toss (1)
   Funny Wonder (1)
8. Alfie the Air Tramp (1)
   Joker (1)
   Wagger the Spare Part (1)

9. Plum and Duff (1)
Comic Cuts (1)
Sergeant Suet (1)
10. Pa Perkins and Percy (1)
Chips (1)
11. Marmaduke and his Ma (1)
later: Marmy and his Ma (1)
Funny Wonder (1)
12. Dad Walker and Wally (1)
Larks (1)
13. Smiler and Smudge (1)
Butterfly (1)
Carraway College (1)
14. Dickie Duffer (1)
Joker (1)
(or *Chips*) (1)
Doctor Doughnut (1)
15. Billy Bunter (1)
Bessie Bunter (1)
Greyfriars (1)
The Magnet (1)
Knockout (1)
Frank Richards (1)
Charles Hamilton (1)
16. Stonehenge Kit (1)
King Kongo (1)
Glam (1)
G. Whizz (Whizzy) (1)
Knockout (1)
17. Ronnie Roy the Rubber Boy (1)
Wonder (1)
18. Homeless Hector (1)
Moonlight Moggie (1)
Chips (1)
19. Our Ernie, Mrs Entwhistle's Little Lad (1)
Knockout (1)
Charlie (1)

Total: 60

21: Phrase Daze

1. Mrs Mop (1)
2. The Diver (1)
3. Sam Scram (1)
4. Signor Soso (1)
5. Mona Lott (1)
6. Miss Hotchkiss (1)
7. Banjulayo (1)
8. Cecil (1)
9. Colonel Chinstrap (1)
10. The Salesman (1)
    (He always had a different name. For example, if he sold items to dust you down, he was 'Michael Osebrush!') (1)
11. Lord Waterlogged (1)
12. Svenson the Svede (1)
13. Commander Highprice (1)
14. Flying-Officer Kite (1)
15. Eric 'Heart-throb' Barker (1)
16. Herr Crow (1)
17. *HMS Waterlogged* (1) later known as *Waterlogged Spa* (1)
18. Jack Warner (1)
19. Arthur Askey (1)
20. Bill Kerr (1)
21. Harry Tate (1)
22. Cyril Fletcher (1)
23. George Doonan (1)
24. Richard Murdoch (1)
25. Old Mother Riley (1) (Arthur Lucan) (1)
26. Frank Randle (1)
27. Ted Ray (1)
28. Tony Hancock (1)
29. Frankie Howerd (1)
30. Tommy Trinder (1)
31. Ivy (1)
    Ray's A Laugh (1)
32. Big Bill Campbell (1)
    Rocky Mountain Rhythm (1)
    (Extra Nostalgia Point if you remembered Tommy Handley used to say it somewhat satirically in *Itma*) (1)
33. Sam Costa (1)
    Much Binding in the Marsh (1)
34. Tosh (1)

Stand Easy (1)

35. Wallace (1)
    Mr Muddlecombe JP (1)
36. Mr Growser (1)
    Toytown (1)
37. Mr Grice (1)
    Howdy Folks (1)
    (played by Douglas Young, extra Nostalgia point for knowing that) (1)
38. Old Ebenezer (1)
    The Old Town Hall (1)
39. The Natives (1)
    Stand Easy (1)
40. Wal (1)
    Take It From Here (1)
41. Haver and Lee (1)
    Danger Men at Work (1)
42. Mr Bygraves (Max) (1)
    Educating Archie (1)

Total: 59

22: Song Throng

1. Leslie Sarony (1)
2. Bobby Howes (1)
3. Lupino Lane (1)
4. Len Bermon (1)
5. Arthur Riscoe (1)
6. Jack Buchanan (1)
7. Maurice Chevalier (1)
8. Stanley Lupino (1)
9. George Elrick (1)
10. Jackie Hunter (1)
11. Vic Oliver (1)
12. Elsie Carlisle (1)
13. Betty Driver (1)
14. Cicely Courtneidge (1)
15. Evelyn Laye (1)
16. Phyllis Robins (1)

17. Billy Williams (1)
18. G. H. Elliott (1)
19. Randolph Sutton (1)
20. George Formby (1)
21. Harry Lauder (1)
22. Will Fyffe (1)
23. Harry Champion (1)
24. Charles Coburn (1)
25. George Robey (1)
26. Charles Penrose (1)
27. Marie Kendall (1)
28. Vesta Victoria (1)
29. Ella Shields (1)
30. Hetty King (1)
31. Lily Morris (1)
32. Florrie Forde (1)
33. Nellie Wallace (1)
34. Marie Lloyd (1)
35. Clarice Mayne (1)

Total: 35

23: Who's Who

1. Richard Goolden (1)
   The Old Town Hall (1)
2. Syd Walker (1)
   Band Waggon (1)
3. Horace Percival (1)
   Itma (1)
4. Hugh Morton (1)
   Welcome All (1)
5. Vic Oliver (1)
   Hi Gang (1)
6. Joy Nichols (1)
   Take It From Here (1)
7. Denis Goodwin (1)
   Hello Playmates (1)
8. Robbie Vincent (1)
   Happidrome (1)

9. Dick Emery (1)
   Educating Archie (1)
10. Dick Bentley (1)
   Take It From Here (1)
11. Doris Nichols (1)
   Danger Men At Work (1)
12. Doris Rogers (1)
   Life With The Lyons (1)
13. Spike Milligan (1)
14. Peter Sellers (1)
15. Peter Sellers (1)
16. Spike Milligan (1)
17. Spike Milligan (1)
18. Peter Sellers (1)
19. Spike Milligan (1)
20. Spike Milligan (1)
21. Peter Sellers (1)
22. Peter Sellers (1)

Total: 34

24: Title Fight

1. Monday Night at Eight (1)
2. Archie's The Boy (1)
3. It's That Sand Again (1)
4. The Goon Show (1)
5. The Dales (1)
6. Ted Ray Time (1)
7. Stand Easy (1)
8. Danger Men Still At Work (1)
9. Abbott and Costello Meet Frankenstein (1)
10. The Oxbow Incident (1)
11. Gaslight (1)
12. House of Horrors (1)
13. Jim Thorpe, All-American (1)
14. The View From Pompey's Head (1)
15. Aaron Slick From Punkin Crick (1)
16. Li'l Abner (1)
17. Saskatchewan (1)

18. Callaway Went Thataway (1)
19. A Tale of Five Cities (1)
20. Barnacle Bill (1)
21. The Two Faces of Dr Jekyll (1)
22. Dracula (1)
23. Fanatic (1)
24. Pimpernel Smith (1)
25. Mother Riley Meets the Vampire (1)
26. Quatermass and the Pit (1)
27. A Matter of Life and Death (1)
28. Where No Vultures Fly (1)
29. The Family Way (1)
30. Sky West and Crooked (1)
31. Morgan (1)
32. Only Two Can Play (1)
33. The Birth of a Nation (1)
34. Satan Met a Lady (1)
    (Yes, we know it was called 'The Maltese Falcon' in 1941 but this was the original version in 1936).
35. The Hounds of Zaroff (1)
36. Curse of the Werewolf (1)
37. Carry On Nurse (1)
38. The Story of Temple Drake (1)

Total: 38

25: Big Sig

1. hear chimes
   take easy
   fireside
   Radio Times
   on the air (10)
2. go away
   stay maybe
   fun
   begun
   laughter
   minute packed (9)

3. Educating Archie
   job anyone
   spelling
   clue
   three sevens
   twenty-two
   problem child
   Educating Archie (13)
4. take trip
   wow
   pack grip
   starting (6)
5. Ignorance Bliss
   folly wise
   better ignorant (6)
6. Ring bell bang drum
   Sound horn shoot gun
   Boys studio
   carpet yourself (12)
7. Happidrome
   show
   tip us
   where go (6)
8. Old Town Hall
   greeting
   Old Town Hall
   meeting
   jolly gay
   pay
   drive troubles (13)
9. *Itma:* It's That Man Again (1)
10. *Hoop-la!* (1)
11. *Much Binding in the Marsh* (1)
12. *Here's Wishing You Well Again* (1)
13. *Shipmates Ashore* ('Sailor Who Are You Dreaming Of Tonight?') (2)
14. *Petticoat Lane* (1)
15. *Ray's A Laugh* (1)

Total: 83

26: Pic Trick

1. Abbott and Costello Meet Captain Kidd (1)
2. Ticket to Tomahawk (1)
3. Down Memory Lane (1)
4. It Always Rains on Sunday (1)
5. Action of the Tiger (1)
6. George and Margaret (1)
7. Paul Temple's Triumph (1)
8. Appointment with Venus (1)
9. The Adventures of PC 49 (1)
10. The Barretts of Wimpole Street (1)
11. I'll Walk Beside You (1)
12. The Angel Who Pawned Her Harp (1)
13. Androcles and the Lion (1)
14. Dance With Me Henry (1)
15. Adam and Evelyn (1)
16. I Know Where I'm Going (1)
17. Heaven Is Round the Corner (1)
18. My Wife's Lodger (1)
19. Prehistoric Women (1)
20. Alice in Wonderland (1)
21. I Married a Monster From Outer Space (1)

Total: 21

27: Tec Check

1. Hugh Morton (or Peter Coke) (1) (2 for both)
2. Noel Johnson (or Duncan Carse) (1) (2 for both)
3. S. J. Warmington (1)
4. Carleton Hobbes (1)
5. Brian Reece (1)
6. John Bentley (or Anthony Hulme) (1) (2 for both)
7. Don Stannard (1)
8. Gordon Harker (1)
9. Basil Rathbone (or Arthur Wontner) (1) (2 for both)
10. Brian Reece (1)
11. Ralph Bellamy (1)
12. Warner Oland (1)

13. William Powell (1)
14. Warren William (1)
15. Chester Morris (1)
16. George Sanders (1)
17. Hugh Sinclair (1)
18. Roger Moore (1)
19. Dorothy L. Sayers (1)
20. Agatha Christie (1)
21. John P. Marquand (1)
22. Michael Arlen (1)
23. Ian Fleming (1)
24. Francis Durbridge (1)
25. Erle Stanley Gardner (1)
26. S.S. Van Dine (1)
27. Leslie Charteris (1)
28. Edward J. Mason (1)
29. Dick Powell (1)
30. Humphrey Bogart (1)
31. Robert Montgomery (1)
32. George Montgomery (1)
33. James Garner (1)
34. Philip Marlowe (1)
35. Raymond Chandler (1)
36. Farewell My Lovely was called Murder My Sweet (1)
37. The High Window was called The Brasher Doubloon (1)
38. Farewell My Lovely was filmed as The Falcon Takes Over (1)
39. The High Window was filmed as Time to Kill (1)
40. The Falcon (1)
41. Michael Shayne (1)
42. Boston Blackie (1)
43. Charlie Chan (1)
44. Paul Temple (1)
45. Bulldog Drummond (1)
46. Perry Mason (1)
47. Hildegarde Withers (1)
48. Miss Marple (1)
49. Dick Barton (1)
50. Inspector Hornleigh (1)
51. The Toff (1)
52. George E. Stone (1)
53. Mantan Moreland (1)
54. Joy Shelton (1)

55. Claude Allister (1)
56. Claire Dodd (1)
57. James Gleason (1)
58. Stringer Davis (1)
59. George Forde (1)
60. Alastair Sim (1)
61. Roddy Hughes (1)
62. No, it wasn't Myrna Loy. She played William Powell's wife, and he played Nick Charles, not the Thin Man. That was our deliberate mistake! If you spotted it, one point; and if you also named the actor who played the Thin Man as Edward Ellis, award yourself a bonus of five Nostalgia Points! (1) (5)

Total: 71

28: Bill Thrill

1. Max Miller (1)
2. Billy Bennett (1)
3. George Robey (1)
4. Revnell and West (1)
5. Claude Dampier (1)
6. Bennett and Williams (1)
7. Norman Long (1)
8. Mr Murgatroyd and Mr Winterbottom (1)
9. Kardomah (1)
10. Oliver Wakefield (1)
11. Donald Peers (1)
12. Arthur Tracy (1)
13. Leslie Holmes (1)
14. Mel Torme (1)
15. Ivor Moreton and Dave Kaye (1)
16. Randolph Sutton (1)
17. Jimmie Rodgers (1)
18. G. H. Elliott (1)
19. G. H. Chirgwin (1)
20. Carmen Miranda (1)

Total: 20

29: Strip Trip (No. 2)

1. Belinda (1)
   Belinda Blue-Eyes (1)
2. Penny (1)
   The Chirrups (1)
   George Davies (1)
   (If you remembered that 'Our Dumb Blonde' was originally drawn by Arthur Ferrier, award yourself an extra Nostalgia Point) (1)
3. Fritz (1)
   Georgie Porgie (1)
4. Susie (1)
   Norman Pett (1)
5. Beelzebub Jones (1)
6. Just Jake (1)
   Eric (1)
7. Captain Reilly-Ffoull (1)
   Arntwee Hall (1)
   Maida Grannitt (1)
8. Dot and Carrie (1)
   Mr Spillikin (1)
   J. H. Horrabin (1)
9. The Flutters (1)
   Bert Cert (1)
   Brenda (1)
10. Ruggles (1)
    John (1)
    (Julian, of course, was Maisie's husband and is out of picture)
11. Pop (1)
    Gog (1)
12. Dawn (1)
    Karen (1)
13. Sooty (1)
    Harry Corbett (1)
14. Teddy Tail (1)
    Douglas Duck (1)
    Mrs Whisker (1)
    Daily Mail (1)
15. Eb and Flo (1)
    The People
16. Pip, Squeak and Wilfred
    The Gugnuncs (1)

(Full name: The Wilfredian Order of Gugnuncs. Extra Nostalgia Point if you got that!) (1)

17. A. B. Payne (1)

Total: 40

30: Number Lumber Number Two

1. 23½ Hours Leave (1)
2. 2000 Women (1)
3. 60 Glorious Years (1)
4. 2 Years Before the Mast (1)
5. 1 Of Our Aircraft Is Missing (1)
6. 13 Rue Madeleine (1)
7. 40 Little Mothers (1)
8. 6 Shootin' Sheriff (1)
9. 20 Mule Team (1)
10. 100 Men and a Girl (1)
11. 50 Roads to Town (1)
12. 40,000 Horsemen (1)
13. 12 O'Clock High (1)
14. 10 Gentlemen From West Point (1)
15. 3 Caballeros (1)
16. 4 Faces West (1)
17. 9 Lives Are Not Enough (1)
18. 7 Keys to Baldpate (1)
19. 5 Graves to Cairo (1)
20. 16 Fathoms Deep (1)
21. Leslie Sarony and Leslie Holmes (2)
22. Larry, Curly and Moe (3)
    Larry Fine, Jerry Howard, Moe Howard (3)
23. Groucho, Chico, Harpo, Zeppo (4)
    Julius, Leonard, Adolph, Herbert (4)
24. Characters in a novel by Margaret Sidney (1)
    Filmed by Columbia in 1940 with Edith Fellows (1)
    and Charles Peck, Tommy Bond, Jimmy Leake, Dorothy Seese
    (If you got them right you are Philip Jenkinson, so no marks!)
25. A popular vocal group in the forties (1)

26. Happy (1), Grumpy (1), Sleepy (1), Sneezy (1), Dopey (1), Doc (1), Bashful (1).

Total: 46

31: Series Queries

1. Penny Singleton (1)
   Arthur Lake (1)
   Bumstead (1)
   Alexander (1)
   Cookie (1)
2. Hardy (1)
   Lewis Stone (1)
   Lionel Barrymore (1)
   Mickey Rooney (1)
   Andy (1)
   Polly Benedict (1)
   Ann Rutherford (1)
   Fay Holden (1)
3. East Side Kids (1)
   Bowery Boys (1)
   Dead End (1)
   Monogram (1)
   Leo Gorcey (1)
   Huntz Hall (1)
   Slip Mahoney (2)
   Sach Debussy Jones (2)
   Louie's Sweet Shop (1)
4. Max Brand (1)
   Kildare (1)
   Lew Ayres (1)
   Gillespie (1)
   Lionel Barrymore (1)
   Laraine Day (1)
   Richard Quine (1)
   Keye Luke (1)
   James Craig (1)
   Van Johnson (regular) (1)

5. Universal (1)
   Basil Rathbone (1)
   Nigel Bruce (1)
   Moriarty (1)
   George Zucco (1)
   Lionel Atwill (1)
   Henry Daniell (1)
   Alan Mowbray (1)
   Dennis Hoey (1)
   Lestrade (1)
   Mary Gordon (1)
   Hudson (1)

Total: 44

32: Paper Caper

1. Evelyn Home (1)
2. Collie Knox (1)
3. Bip Pares (1)
4. Reg Whiteley (1)
5. Nat Gubbins (1)
6. Irene Veal (1)
7. C. A. Lejeune (1)
8. Jonah Barrington (1)
9. William Hickey (1)
10. Trevor Wignall (1)

Total: 10

33: Sport Short

1. Tommy Farr (1)
2. Primo Carnera (1)
3. Max Schmelling (1)
4. Steve Donoghue (1)
5. Knute Rockne (1)
6. Bluey Wilkinson (1)
7. Malcolm Campbell (1)

8. Don Bradman (1)
9. Jack Johnson (1)
10. Joe Louis (1)

Total: 10

34: Ad Mad

1. Guinness (1)
2. Barratt (1)
3. Bravington (1)
4. Kruschen (1)
5. Bovril (1)
6. Shell (1)
7. Bisto (1)
8. Minor (1)
9. Elasto (1)
10. Lyon-ch (1)
11. The Bennett College (1)
12. Kensitas (1)
13. Rowntree's Gums (1)
14. Pelmanism (1)
15. Erasmic (1)
16. Horlicks (1)
17. Gibb's Dentifrice (1)
18. Oxo (1)
19. Nestle's Milk (1)
20. The Pickwick, the Owl and the Waverley Pen (1)
21. Force (1)
22. Carter's Little Liver Pills (1)
23. Ovaltine (1)
24. Betox (1)

Total: 24

35: Flicks Mix

1. Lynn Bari (1)
2. Nan Grey (1)

3. Wendy Barrie (1)
4. Jean Parker (1)
5. Priscilla Lane (1)
6. Julie Bishop (1)
7. Ellen Drew (1)
8. Evelyn Ankers (1)
9. Ruth Hussey (1)
10. Ann Savage (1)
11. Leon Errol (1)
12. Pedro de Cordoba (1)
13. Jerry Colonna (1)
14. Tom Neal (1)
15. Chester Clute (1)
16. Erich Von Stroheim (1)
17. Andrew Toombes (1)
18. Edward Norris (1)
19. John Litel (1)
20. Jerome Cowan (1)

Total: 20

36: Strip Trip (No. 3)

1. Tin Can Tommy (1)
2. Waddles (1)
3. Charlie Chutney (1)
4. Nero and Zero (1)
5. Freddy (1)
6. Rip Van Wink (1)
7. Pansy Potter (1)
8. Hair Oil Hal (1)
9. Inky Poo (1)
10. Julius Sneezer (1)
11. Hairy Hugh (1)
12. Polly Wolly Doodle (1)
13. Musso the Wop
14. Cocky Dick (1)
15. Wee Peem (1)
16. Hairy Dan (1)
17. Handy Sandy (1)

18. Big Fat Joe (1)
19. Old Ma Murphy (1)
20. Big Heep (1)
21. Merry Marvo (1)
22. Jimmy Watson (1)
23. Little Jim Jolly (1)
24. Mickey (1)
25. Suck'Em and See (1)
26. Rosie, Hairpin Huggins, Skinny Lizzie, Scrapper Smith, Happy Hutton, Snitchy, Snatchy, Gertie the Goat (8)
27. Lord Marmaduke of Bunkerton (1)
28. Carl 'Alfalfa' Switzer, Scotty Beckett, Darla Hood, Billy Thomas, Patsy May, Porky Lee, Spanky McFarland, Buckwheat Thomas, Pete the Pup (9)
29. Hal Roach (1)
30. Dudley D. Watkins (1)
31. Tiger Tim, Jumbo the Elephant, Jacko the Monkey, Fido the Dog, Bobby the Bear, Joey the Parrot, Porkyboy the Pig, Georgie the Giraffe (8) and an Ostrich (1) whose name is so elusive that if you know it, write and tell me and I'll personally send you Ten Nostalgia Points!
32. The Hippo Girls (1)
33. *Playbox* (1)

Total: 56

37: Hero Zero

1. The Wolf of Kabul (1)
2. Big Bad Wolff (1)
3. Solo Solomon (1)
4. Captain Justice (1)
5. Strang the Terrible (1)
6. Sexton Blake (1)
7. The Big Stiff (1)
8. Black Sapper (1)
9. The Laughing Buccaneer (1)
10. Dixon Hawke (1)
11. The Blackfriars Phantom (1)
12. Colwyn Dane (1)

13. Mad Carew (1)
14. Rockfist Rogan (1)
15. Fireworks Flynn (1)

Total: 15

38: Phrase Craze

1. Laurel and Hardy (1)
2. Sydney Howard (1)
3. Claude Hulbert (1)
4. Joe E. Brown (1)
5. Harold Lloyd (1)
6. Wheeler and Woolsey (1)
7. Claude Dampier (1)
8. George Formby (1)
9. Abbott and Costello (1)

Total: 9

39: Finale Parlay

1. Uncle Mac (Derek McCullough) (1) plus (1)
2. Sandy Powell (1)
3. Wilfred Pickles (1)
4. Carroll Gibbons (1)
5. Geraldo (1)
6. Clay Keyes (1)
7. Henry Hall (1)
8. Syd Walker (1)
9. Bernard Braden (1)
   as 'Uncle Gabby' (1)
10. Stanelli and his Stag Party (1)
    (extra Nostalgia Point if you remembered the tune!) (1)

Total: 13
Grand N.Q. Total: 1250

Nostalgia is Good for You

A few thoughts from your panellist, Bob Monkhouse

Time marches on and I, for one, feel trampled. It's age, I suppose. That biological urge has turned into an occasional nudge. I'm getting to the stage when, as the old gag says, I don't make love on Saturdays in case it rains on Sundays. And there's been another change . . .

The future, which once seemed so sweet, daunts me with the sourness of its pollution, parking, population, and pop. And the past – *my* past – has taken on a magic it never had before.

Increasingly, in those quiet, meditative moments that life allows us today . . . watching the pattern of your coloured St Michael underpants swirling in the corner coinamatic, or spending 24 hours of your eight-day holiday in the airport lounge at Gatwick, with your toothbrush packed and most of your polystyrene sandwich glued to your teeth . . . more and more, I find, I review the past. And the sum of my life so far is a series of recollections. Some peculiarly my own. Some shared. Probably with you.

Remember dancing? I mean, *real* dancing, back in the days when it was smooching set to the music of Geraldo. You just held her very close and tried to get behind her without getting round her.

And from smooching, you graduated to snogging and, eventually, to 'heavy petting'. In my society, that meant feeling the outside of bra in the back row of the Odeon. In those days, the only 'teen-age protest' was her saying 'no'!

Remember when air was clean and sex was dirty? When Hollywood stardom depended on how good a girl looked *inside* a sweater? Remember when . . . ?

'Ah, happy days!' chorused Big-Hearted Arthur and Stinker, and how right they were. Precious because we never knew their value. Joyful because the memory of pain fades. Full of wonder because so were we.

It's no use boring the young with your own youth. Nostalgia is a self-indulgence with a capital self. You can share it as a game, just as you can share this book, with others of your own age group. But don't inflict it on the children. It'll only lead you from fond recollections of when Kensitas offered you 'Four for your friends' to a harangue about the dangers of smoking. *From* your children, I mean.

And you can't pass on the lessons of experience, either. There are only three or four human stories and they go on repeating themselves as fiercely as if they had never happened before. Experience is what you get while you're looking for something else. Today's young people will gather theirs while they pursue the marvels of *Oz*, Jethro Tull and balanced ecology.

And some day, incredible as it seems now, all that will be their nostalgia. Doesn't bear thinking about, does it?

Bob Monkhouse